William Halstead is a writer from Yorkshire, England. He initially worked in finance for many years after leaving college, before turning to writing and blogging. In July 2021 he set up a community interest company called Laid Bear Recovery, to help people with gambling and mental health issues.

William Halstead

A House in the Countryside

Living Gamble Free and Happy

Austin Macauley Publishers™
London • Cambridge • New York • Sharjah

All of the events in this memoir are true to the best of author's memory. The views expressed in this memoir are solely those of the author.

A CIP catalogue record for this title is available from the British Library.

ISBN 9781398422599 (Paperback)
ISBN 9781398422605 (ePub e-book)

www.austinmacauley.com

First Published 2022
Austin Macauley Publishers Ltd®
1 Canada Square
Canary Wharf
London
E14 5AA

Table of Contents

For every lovely human being who has stood by me.

For a long time, as negative as this sounds, I'd say gambling was the most exciting thing in my life. The thrill and adrenaline rush from gambling wasn't comparable to anything else. And that's what addiction is, that's why it happens, that's why it exists. But in the long term, the addiction eats away at every other positive in your life, until the only positive is when you're getting the fix. Everything else falls apart. Soon enough, the addiction is the only thing that ceases the anxiety of your shit existence. It's a sad and lonely place. It's unsustainable. This can't go on forever. Eventually, it becomes too much.

Gambling and Mental Health

'It's not just gambling with money; it's gambling with lives.'

What is mental health?

What is addiction? Do I have an addiction?

Is there a link between addiction and mental health?

What do 12 years of heavy gambling do to a person?

Am I alone in life? Am I the only person with these problems?

Is there a way for me to change my path or am I pretty much fucked?

Will this all end in my premature death? Or locked up in a mental institution?

Several years ago, I wouldn't have asked these questions. I certainly couldn't have answered them. I perhaps still can't fully understand to this day what I have endured. But what I do have, is a much better understanding of myself and what I need from life. What makes me happy. And that's what is surely most important?

What Is This Book?

True.
Concise.
A memoir.
Sad.
Happy.
Funny.
Unbelievable.
Informative.
Honest.
And proof that things and people can change for the better.

This book started with a blank piece of A4 paper on which I began to write down my thoughts and feelings after many years of gambling. My addiction was slowly killing the person I was, and I knew I needed to change something drastically. The eventuality of wanting to 'fix myself' but feeling hopeless when I couldn't was awful. I always said I could give up, but truth is, by the end I was terrified I couldn't stop. Am I a leopard, unable to change my spots? Were gambling and mental health problems part of my innate nature, my genetic make-up? This thought was ruthlessly chipping away at what was left of my existence. The addict would always overpower me. Because that's what it was for me. I was me – funny, weird, affectionate, mischievous, nerdy. But I was also sharing my life with an addict who had slowly grown stronger as my own self-worth had grown weaker. This person was the opposite of everything I am. My addiction fed mental health problems and I was eventually, and now I know inevitably, caught up by serious depression and anxiety.

Recovery is a battle. A battle that has become easier simply through knowledge. Learning about my addiction and subsequent problems is what has truly helped me. I don't believe the addiction can be *cured – an addict is an addict is an addict*. But it can be beaten down by the power of understanding it and the realisation of why it can't be allowed to win. For many years, I tried to ignore the addiction, but this wasn't helping. The addiction is fact. I knew I must face it head on.

I've accepted over time that I shouldn't be ashamed of my journey, it's what has shaped me as a person and is a continuous reminder to me of why I don't gamble and why my mental health is so important. With the struggle I've experienced over the last 12 years, I eventually started to realise that I could use this to possibly help other people who are going through similar situations to me, and to make them realise they are not alone – something I felt a lot during my darkest days. For years, I wondered if anyone at all was going through what I was. The more I have researched gambling and addiction for this book, the more I have become aware of the scale of the problem. People may suffer in a variety of ways with gambling, but the inner mechanics of every gambler's brain are the same. And this structure which eventually leads to addiction has lasting negative impacts on mental health in a lot of cases.

The following account will not be a glamourous and comfortable read for many. It will possibly shock even the people who have always been there to support me. I will be giving a brutally honest account – as honest as I can possibly be to help people understand – of my actions and thoughts and what they caused. An open window into the mind of a gambling addict and the further mental illness issues that follow such an addiction. It's hard for others to know what's happened and see the full picture. What is seen is usually the aftermath and consequences of gambling. I hope this will give whoever is interested an insight into this life. A poor life no one should have to lead.

I also want this book to provide people, who are struggling to support someone with gambling and mental health issues, a detailed insight into the problems. This can help to fight this notion that addicts are alone when dealing with their problems. And possibly help stop those who are supporting an addict from feeling helpless.

What Isn't This Book?

This book is not a lecture to everyone who has ever gambled. There are a lot of people out there who can gamble, have fun and walk away. I am not one of those people. There are, however, thousands like me. I'm now 31 years old, and after 12 years of battling this ruthless disease, I feel it's time to tell my story. Gambling and mental health battles feel like 'the elephant in the room' at times, but the truth is, it's silently destroying lives. I want others to realise that if they think they need help, they should seek it out like I eventually did.

What worked for me will not necessarily work for everyone who has gambling problems, but what is true, is that anyone who thinks they may be struggling, can stop with the right help and actions. It doesn't have to lead to mental health problems like depression and anxiety. It doesn't have to lead to the destruction of someone's life. A life of debt and failing relationships and all the other shit that accompanies addiction. To never start gambling in the first place, for those susceptible, would be idyllic. However, in today's world where gambling is so accessible and normalised, this seems unlikely.

I like to think this book is me signing off a period of my life. Putting my experiences in a locked box for a time when I might want to look at them again. My life of gambling up to this point has shaped me but it will no longer control me, and this book is a continuous reminder of it.

Sigmund Freud

The renowned Sigmund Freud.

Sigmund Freud was an Austrian neurologist and founder of the technique known as psychoanalysis. Psychoanalysis is the clinical method of treating psychopathology through dialogue between a patient and a psychoanalyst – having a chat, I guess! Though at times his work was provocative, it is without doubt that Freud's thinking has left a lasting mark on psychology, psychiatry and psychotherapy. This guy also knew how to turn a phrase! I have picked out a few quotes from Freud which I thought were interesting and I could relate to. I have put these throughout the book (denoted by an SF) where I felt it was most appropriate. Freud isn't someone I knew much about before studying him for this book. I now know that, for all his famous and crazy ideas, he was an important figure in history. A giant of the thinking world.

Part I – Gambling Addiction

The Beginning

My name is Will and I am a gambling addict. I also struggle with mental health issues. First of all, the gambling. This is where the difficulties began for me.

I haven't admitted my addiction too often over the last 12 years, even though they were spent living my life on the spin of a roulette wheel, the roll of a dice or the kick of a football. I've never had any doubt in my mind that this is what I am. However, I've found that the world gambling created was a secretive and lonely place. One which I hid from most people. Those close family and friends who were aware of my addiction struggled to understand it. Just as much as I struggled to find a way out.

Did my early life suggest I was more susceptible to this destructive disease? I had always had what me and my friends would jokingly call an *addictive personality,* but I'm sure that gambling addiction goes beyond that. Something works differently in a gambling addict's brain, the mechanics are distorted. The draw of 'just one more bet' and nothing outside of the 'gambling bubble' being able to change that. After all, the reason I have lost so much money and time to gambling over the years is that inability to just walk away.

As my counsellor would later enlighten me, gambling began to service a need for me. It was no longer the fun hobby I had experienced when I first started doing it. Gambling now enabled me to function in everyday life, taking my mind off other problems. Much like an alcoholic or a smoker, I was addicted and was continually needing a fix. Along with this was the draw of 'free money' – something I have come to realise doesn't exist except in the mind of an addict.

My First Gamble

'Gambling is the wagering of money or something of value on an event with an uncertain outcome, with the primary intent of winning money or material goods. Wager. Chance. Prize.'

How did it all begin for me? Looking back to the first time I gambled, it was an unassuming act. I certainly didn't think it would end up being a turning point for my life and one which would shape me as a person forever. Do I regret the day? I think it's easy to say that I do, and for a long time, I carried a lot of anger, guilt and shame for what I did. But today, I'm also a great believer that everything we go through happens for a reason. All my experiences in life, good and bad, go towards who I am as a person. If I can learn from my mistakes going forward, then it's not a complete loss. What has happened is now out of my control and can only now be used as an experience and an educator for what happens next. For a gambler, to regret the past and the loss of money is a dangerous mentality. I could spend the rest of my life chasing the tens of thousands of pounds I have lost, but would doing that end positively? I know for a fact it wouldn't.

I have always been interested in watching and playing sports, particularly football. I was born in the late '80s and grew up in the '90s idolising footballers. I was taken to my first football matches by my dad and spent my spare time collecting the Premier League sticker albums. This hobby would later become the basis for my first gamble. I recall being sat in work as an impressionable 18-year-old junior accountant, straight out of sixth form college, and the lads in the office talking about what bets they had put on for the upcoming weekend's football. I shared the office with around 8 other people, and they all happened to be young lads who were interested in football and some in gambling – I never stood a chance! What was a hobby for them, though, would become much more for me.

Having a chat about football over a morning coffee at work was the staple every day. Once gambling was introduced, my curiosity got the better of me. I became excited thinking of the chance of earning 'free money' without doing any work. I was on a modest wage but with a fair amount of what you might call 'disposable income'. I remember thinking I could use my knowledge of football to earn a little extra cash. And so, that weekend I opened my first online gambling account and placed my first bet. I didn't know much about gambling, so deposited £5 into my account and placed a £1 'accumulator' bet. I remember, at the time of doing this I had mentioned it to my dad. He had questioned whether it was a good idea as he knew gambling wasn't necessarily a good habit. I sort of reassured him, and myself, that it wouldn't be a regular thing and my bets would only be a quid here and there. I thought, *What's a few pounds to someone who was earning a wage now*? It was one of the reasons I had gone straight from college to working full-time and missing out on university. I wanted money in my bank account and an apprenticeship in accountancy seemed the ideal way to do this.

By the next weekend's football, I had my first winner. I hadn't been gambling heavy but having lost a few quid in the process, my bets had increased to £5 a time; the first sign that this was going to be more than just a fun pastime. I had selected a variety of football games across the European fixtures on a Sunday afternoon. I remember logging onto my online account that evening and the joy when I realised the bet had come in and I had won £175. My heart skipped a beat when I saw my account balance. I didn't really follow the games at this time; I placed a bet and then checked later on if it had won. As I became more fixated, I would be following games on my phone, and eventually within a few months, I'd be up at all hours in the night sacrificing sleep to follow the football and other sports live.

I told my dad about my £175 win as if to say 'I told you so' – there's a weird sense of 'superiority over others' when a win comes in gambling. Weird because most people know gambling isn't a way to make money. Again, my dad questioned me – 'I thought you were only doing £1 bets?' – I waived it off and said I'd had a couple of winners so had been able to increase my bets. This was a lie, of course, something that later became a regular occurrence for me as a problem gambler – the bottom line was I was hooked. The gambling had been justified; I was a winner. Even in those initial few weeks of gambling, there were worrying signs of what was to come.

During my early months' gambling, 'accumulator' bets were my go-to bet. This involves predicting various sporting outcomes and all must be correct to win the bet. They offer longer odds (the chance of something happening – the less chance, the longer/higher the odds and the greater the reward) due to the higher number of outcomes. Accumulator bets are one of the crafty tools used by bookmakers for profit – a profit that a gambler will rarely see. The thought of winning big money from small bets is very attractive to most people; however, it's pretty clear that it's an awful way to gamble due to the ever-increasing odds and the fact that these odds are balanced away from the gambler in general. It's hard enough to pick one outcome, never mind five or six. Often, I would hear someone complain, 'Aw, I was only one/two game(s) from my accumulator winning!' For me, these bets added a bit of 'spice' to watching the football at the weekend and with my knowledge of football, what could go wrong? Skewed thinking like this was just a steppingstone for what was to follow.

Google Generation

'Gambling – the guaranteed way to get nothing for something.'

There is no doubt that technological advancement over the last ten years has increased the reach of gambling. I rarely walked into a bookmaker to place bets but would spend hours on my laptop or phone doing it. I remember when you could only make phone calls on mobile phones and texts cost 10p or 12p – now you can use gambling apps to place bets of thousands of pounds a time. I also remember computers were huge boxes which were incredibly slow and time on the internet was limited to when my mum wasn't on a phone call to my grandma. Computers now rule the world.

Gambling on sports was soon not enough to get my fix and discovering online casinos took my problems to a whole new level. The amount of money that can be placed on the spin of a roulette wheel or a slot machine is frightening – and it wasn't long before I was maxing out on what I could afford. There is a distinct lack of control over money which is gambled online. Gambling restrictions can be placed on accounts; however, these can easily be turned on and off and are not much use to someone experiencing the problems I was and in the vulnerable state I was in. Ironically, over all the years I have played at online casinos, only once have I been suspended by a company for spending, what they thought, was beyond my means – yes, they were right, but none of the others ever questioned it. They ask 'are you in control' – how is a person who is *out of control* going to answer that? – yes, I'm fine, I can afford this, piss off and let me carry on gambling.

As with the sports betting, the gambling at the online casino had started out controlled and only gradually began to get out of hand. I can remember clearly how it started on a well-known casino site. Roulette, for those who are unfamiliar, is a casino game which involves a wheel of numbers and a ball and betting on certain numbers, certain groups of numbers, the colours red or black, odd or even numbers and high or low numbers. On average, the players will always lose, as with most casino games, due to the house edge. In this game, it is due to the green number zero which brings the total numbers on the wheel to 37 but pay-outs are at odds of 36/1 on a single number. Once I saw the potential for making 'free money' on this game, I was hooked, and a house edge meant nothing to me – that went straight to the back of my mind. I had a decent grasp of probability and odds but would choose to ignore this in favour of the excitement I got from gambling.

The casinos and bookies are great at keeping themselves fresh and exciting to gamblers. It's a way of keeping gamblers hooked – there are lots of varieties of games, new and old, at casinos and new ways to bet on sports. It's what a lot of casinos and bookies base their advertising around – new slots, new ways to bet. When in-play betting (being able to bet on sports as they happen) was first introduced, advertisements were everywhere being shoved down our throats, and still are today. I remember when the game 100/1 roulette first arrived, a game based around a much bigger roulette wheel, and I recall the amount of money I threw away. I was simply drawn in by its design. I was hooked. *Wow, a roulette wheel four times bigger.* It does seem silly to me now when I think about it, but it wasn't to me at the time. It was just another way of gambling.

There was a slot machine based around the War of the Worlds stage show. It will sound gimmicky to most people, but I was drawn in by the music (a magical score from Jeff Wayne), the colours and the bonus rounds. It didn't even feel like gambling at times, clicking away money on the spin of a slot machine. Again, as with roulette, the amount I gambled increased and increased. There was no walking away when I was up either. If I did walk away, I'd be back on within a few hours, looking for that buzz I got from a bonus round or a high stakes win. All throughout my gambling addiction, I would play slots – if I lost money, I'd deposit more money into my gambling account, go over to roulette, and try and double the balance. If I won, I'd be back on the slots again. If I lost, I'd again be depositing money.

Once money was deposited onto an online betting account, it was going to be lost. I almost thought of it as 'Monopoly money' once it had been deposited – it didn't feel real, it didn't feel like the money I worked hard for. The way I threw it away, you'd think it was someone else's money. Gambling with money from a debit card doesn't ever feel like real money. Winning £100 in a casino was much bigger than during online gambling. Visible cash in your hand is much more satisfying. I was never happy with what I had won online, I always wanted more. I would always withdraw winnings online but cancel the pending withdrawal to my bank account because I couldn't wait to gamble again. Often, I would just end up losing this money.

I was struggling to stop. At the time, with almost every online casino, self-excluding was a fairly easy process – but to do this on the hundreds of bookmakers available online, most of which I was a member, was another matter altogether. New companies were popping up all the time due to the solid business model. I don't often hear stories of these companies going bankrupt – it has been the main big players in the gaming industry for years. Self-excluding wasn't the way I was going to stop gambling. There was a deeper issue at play – a gambling addict will always find a way to gamble and the only way to stop is to fix the problem at its most basic form, not cover it up.

The Gambling 'Bubble'

I mention the gambling bubble a lot when talking about my experiences. I can't stress enough how dangerous this was. The reason I probably felt like a different person when gambling was due to this. Disassociating myself from reality and who I really am. The bubble was, at times, thick and difficult to pop. The bubble was impenetrable to the physical world, nothing outside mattered. I lost interest in going out, spending whole days and nights gambling. Hour after hour, I would think about nothing else. I wouldn't look after myself mentally or physically, instead choosing to gamble.

The bubble was impenetrable to the feelings of other people. I didn't think of the hurt I was causing anyone. The bubble was also impenetrable to my own feelings. Anxieties drifted away when I was gambling. Even when outside of the bubble in the 'real world', the thoughts of gambling helped detract from my problems. I would sit at work waiting for the day to end so I could get home, turn my laptop on, and spend the rest of the evening gambling. The thought of gambling was exhilarating. Whether I was happy in life was dependant on whether I was gambling at that time.

What are bubbles eventually known for doing? Yes, they burst. And when my bubble burst, after losing thousands of pounds, was when I would start to suffer. At my worst, I would lose my passion for life, wanting to kill myself. I would see first-hand the pain I had caused other people as I suddenly became aware of what was in front of me. This would repeat itself over and over. Once I was back in the bubble, I'd forget about all the other times it had happened. It was a vicious cycle – gambling to forget problems that originally resulted from gambling.

Remaining outside of the gambling bubble became a priority. Yes, it stopped anxieties initially, but in the end, it would multiply those anxieties by a thousand due to the situation I was left in.

How do I remain outside of the gambling bubble? If this was key to my welfare, it was something I was going to have to find an answer to.

Payday to Payday

'Easy come, easy go.'

Addiction takes many forms, but the one thing that they all have in common is that you could look back to times when you were fully immersed in its relentless grip and not be able to fully comprehend your actions. If I were on the outside looking in, I would think these actions were insane. It would embarrass me if someone saw me doing something like this. I would be ashamed. How can someone be so selfish? Demonstrating such senseless actions. I remember once being in a casino with friends and seeing one guy lose a deposit for a house – all his savings gone in as little as one hour's roulette play. I couldn't believe it as I sat there watching. He looked like he'd headed into the casino with the cash and was already resigned to losing it all. No matter what he won, he just kept playing until it was all gone. Thousands of pounds spun away on the roulette wheel. I didn't know whether to laugh or cry, the sadness of the situation was so extreme. *Thank fuck that's not me who'd just done that*, I thought to myself. Yet deep down, I knew I was the same as this person. The only difference being that I would put on an act when I was with other people.

Within a few years of having my first innocent online sports bet, I was now living life payday to payday. Being sat alone in front of my laptop at midnight on the 25th of each month, refreshing the page, waiting for my salary to enter my bank account so I could gamble – it now seems like a harrowing experience but at the time it was the norm and nothing else infiltrated the bubble that was created through gambling. Over the period I was gambling, I was earning a hard-earned, modest pay and yet most of it was being thrown away.

The trouble I had is that I'd lose a massive amount gambling but two weeks later, I would have put the loss behind me and started gambling again. It's not that I'd forgotten the loss, I chose not to think about it. It is quite common to think you only ever remember the wins, but I also remember a lot of the losses now. These losses were accountable for such grave times in my life that they're not easy to forget. They scarred me, but I was also able to temporarily suppress them and continue gambling. This in itself was a way to forget my problems from gambling. I also think the other reason I remember the losses is because the wins were few and far between. Yes, I had short-term wins and 'streaks' but I would soon end these by gambling incessantly and chasing losses to the brink of debt. This would eventually catch up with me when losing my salary every month wasn't enough.

One memory which reflects how gambling ruled my life was a holiday I was going on with some friends. I'd been saving up for a while and was looking forward to it. I was gambling heavily around that time and my bank account was a fragile mess which could barely take the strain of my addiction. I had the bank ringing me up, asking if I was happy depositing such large sums into my online gambling accounts. It was so bad, it was highlighted as possible fraud on the bank's detection system! One night, I was gambling on roulette and lost pretty much all the money I had. At a stage like this, I would become frustrated at having to walk away with nothing left. I was on the verge of not being able to go on holiday, I was deep in debt and had nothing. I was desperate and happened to notice I had £20 left in one of my gambling accounts. I think it must have been from when I had been gambling previously and I had lost so much I hadn't bothered to gamble this 'small amount' leftover. With the £20, I went back to roulette and managed to get back the money I had lost and was able to make the holiday. Hundreds of pounds made from £20. These moments though are the most dangerous, when you feel invincible. This all just adds to what will happen in the future – you take this feeling of invincibility and gamble again. Situations like this feed the addiction further. These thoughts I carry into the next time I gamble are all based on the time I won, not when I'd nearly lost the lot with a holiday on the line. Short term, I could go on holiday. Long term, how many holidays would I fritter away in the future?

The continual thought process throughout gambling is 'this is my time to land the big win and walk away.' What I thought this 'big win' was is anybody's guess. I have won large five-figure sums in the past and still not walked away. Maybe I withdrew a lot of it from my gambling account, but it would always end up being put back in eventually. I would feel relief briefly when I didn't have access to money. Maybe I was waiting for my bank to process a withdrawal. As soon as it hit my bank account, however, I couldn't stop myself from putting it back into gambling.

I would set targets of what I wanted to win while playing but I was also affected by an odd sense of obsessive compulsion. Setting targets in my head. *If I get to £1,000, I can walk away.* Of course, £950 wasn't enough. I would continue to gamble and often, lose the £950. Again, the balance in my account would feel like Monopoly money, I was comfortable gambling large amounts. After a while, this became more stressful for me as my money worries deepened. I know now, the targets I set were pointless. Even if I reached my target, I would carry on. Always wanting that bit more until what I had was gone.

My bank account during a heavy gambling month was sickening to look at. Tens of thousands of pounds of transactions would go through my bank account – ins and outs which could be thousands more than what I was earning in a month. If I look back, I can see months where as much as £50,000 was moving through my bank account in a month. To say that makes me feel sick is an understatement. I remember having as much as £16k of winnings in my bank which had been built up over a month of gambling. I didn't have any debt at this point in my life, so this was a lot of money. £16k just burning a hole in my pocket and waiting to be gambled again, which, of course, it was.

Working for the Weekend

After years of gambling, I became a robot in work. I lacked motivation and drive for a job I once enjoyed. As an accountant, it's hard to not think about money and I was at work physically but not mentally. I wasn't interested in being there due to my mind being preoccupied. Firstly, it was due to gambling, then for mental health reasons.

I remember times when I would gamble on my phone at work, downloading gambling apps to play roulette, having a go on the slots or doing some sports betting. Gambling was all I thought about 24/7. I look back and think how unprofessional it was, but it reflects how desperate my situation was at the time. Gambling in those moments was everything to me. It decided whether I was happy or sad, had money or was penniless. The quick changing moods and severe ups and downs would impact negatively on my mental health.

Can you imagine the picture? Sitting at work, at my desk or in the toilet, when I should be working, spinning the roulette wheel or a slot machine. Sometimes I'd even have sports bets on the go, random basketball games in Indonesia or football matches in Australia. I'd be sat, constantly checking scores.

If I had a large loss one day, my mind would be on this and work didn't matter. It was awful setting off to work on a morning feeling like life was pointless. Sat in the car in silence thinking about my problems then having to put on an act at work like everything was fine.

My way of earning a guaranteed income was taking a back seat to the gambling.

20 Questions - Gambling Addiction

It took a long time to accept I had a problem. Here are twenty questions that could be asked to determine whether someone is a problem gambler. Not all encompassing but without doubt gives a good overall idea.

Questions

1. Have you ever taken time off work or university so that you can gamble?
2. Has gambling ever made your home life unhappy?
3. Has gambling affected your reputation with friends and colleagues?
4. Have you ever felt remorse after gambling?
5. Have you ever gambled to win money with which to pay debts or otherwise solve financial difficulties?
6. Has gambling caused a decrease in your ambition or efficiency?
7. After losing, do you feel you must return as soon as possible and win back your losses?
8. After a win, do you have a strong urge to return and win more?
9. Do you often gamble until your last pound has gone?
10. Have you ever borrowed to finance your gambling?
11. Have you ever sold anything to finance gambling?

12. Are you reluctant to use 'gambling money' for normal expenditures?
13. Has gambling ever made you careless of the welfare of yourself or your family?
14. Do you ever gamble longer than you have planned?
15. Do you gamble to escape worry or trouble?
16. Have you ever committed or considered committing an illegal act to finance gambling?
17. Has gambling caused you to have difficulty sleeping?
18. Do arguments, disappointments or frustrations create within you an urge to gamble?
19. Do you ever have an urge to celebrate any good fortune by a few hours of gambling?
20. Have you ever considered self-destruction or suicide because of your gambling?

My Answers

1. Yes 2. Yes 3. Yes 4. Yes 5. Yes 6. Yes 7. Yes 8. Yes 9. Yes 10. Yes 11. Yes 12. Yes 13. Yes 14. Yes 15. Yes 16. Yes 17. Yes 18. Yes 19. Yes 20. Yes

I could answer YES to every single one of these questions at some point over the last 12 years.

Even if someone is only answering YES to 5%, I'd say that is enough of an issue. Gambling should in no way impact negatively on life.

Answering YES to at least 7 is the sign of a compulsive gambler according to the survey (Gamblers Anonymous).

NHS - 9 questions

The NHS has similar questions but a different scoring system to ascertain a problem gambler.

1. Do you bet more than you can afford to lose?
2. Do you need to gamble with larger amounts of money to get the same feeling?
3. Have you tried to win back money you have lost (chasing losses)?
4. Have you borrowed money or sold anything to get money to gamble?
5. Have you wondered whether you have a problem with gambling?
6. Has your gambling caused you any health problems, including feelings of stress or anxiety?
7. Have other people criticised your betting or told you that you had a gambling problem (regardless of whether you thought it was true)?
8. Has your gambling caused any financial problems for you or your household?
9. Have you ever felt guilty about the way you gamble or what happens when you gamble?

I will answer each of these separately as it is a score-based system used by the NHS. Score 0 for each time you answer ‘never’, score 1 each time you answer ‘sometimes’, score 2 each time you answer ‘most of the time’, score 3 for each time you answer ‘almost always’. If your total score is 8 or higher, you may be a problem gambler.

1. Score 3 – I would bet more than I can afford to lose every time when gambling, increasing my debts.
2. Score 3 – When I first started gambling, it was mainly small amounts but increased with time to get that same feeling.
3. Score 3 – I would try to win back money I lost every time when gambling, never accepting losses.
4. Score 3 – I have borrowed lots of money to gamble with.
5. Score 3 – From early on, I have thought I am a problem gambler.
6. Score 3 – I am now seeing serious signs of mental health issues due to gambling.
7. Score 3 – My friends and family who are aware of my gambling and know I have a gambling problem.
8. Score 3 – Gambling has caused me massive problems financially with big debts created.
9. Score 3 – I have always felt guilt, anger and remorse from the gambling I have done.

I can honestly say that is the most successful test result of my life! – 100%! 27 out of a possible 27!

I Have a Problem – What Now?

Even the day I realised I had a problem, it didn't curtail my habits. Accepting the problem, they say, is the first and most important step. The next step for me was much harder. I have always in some way, maybe subconsciously most of the time, accepted I have a problem – to me that was clear. I knew what I was doing wasn't normal and this became apparent during the early years I spent gambling. The fast pace at which it went from fun to necessity.

Can I completely stop? Should I completely stop? Or should I just practice moderation and only gamble on certain things I can stay in control of? What if I can never stop and I'm helpless? I now know that moderation isn't a possibility for me. Any venture into gambling for me will not end well. I'll always take it too far and end up losing lots of money. I always thought the temptations throughout life would be too much to stop completely. A poker night with mates, a flutter on the Grand National, a lottery ticket at the weekend or a quick game on the pub gambling machine. I look at it now and I know it's just not worth it. Stop completely now and be thankful later. Deciding that my issues were too big and that I needed to stop gambling completely was an easy choice to make. Being able to stop was going to be a lot more challenging.

Gambling to Me

What words do I associate with gambling?

When times were good…

Exciting. Thrilling. Adrenaline inducing. Heart racing. Hobby. A high. Free money. Profit. Winning. Money. Money. Money.

The bad times…

Scary. Gut-wrenching. Self-hatred. Nerve-wracking. Not free money. Monopoly money. Sickening. Heart-breaking. Addictive. Harmful. Alcohol. Suicidal. Stressful. Anxious.

Depressed. Helpless. Gambling fallacy. Chasing. Loss. Can't stop. Want to stop. Terrifying. Selfish. Poor. Lapses. Relapses. Losing. Loser. Losing more. Just shit. Really shit.

A lot more negatives than positives. The positives tend to be a lie anyway – things you tell yourself to excuse the addiction.

The cursed beauty of gambling is that its utterly engrossing. Life problems evaporate into thin air in that moment when you're waiting for the ball to drop onto the roulette wheel or celebrating a goal at the death of a football match. It's not until the dust has settled that the repulsive underbelly of gambling becomes apparent. That's why it's so important to remember these times when it's all gone horribly wrong. I do, and I'm not afraid to, remind myself of these dark periods. Why don't I gamble?

Physical Symptoms

There are a lot of physical symptoms that I associate with gambling, not just mental problems. Things that were apparent whenever I was gambling heavy. On the verge of losing everything. Nausea, heart racing, sickness, insomnia.

When gambling, my heart would be racing, akin to working out at the gym. On a few occasions while gambling, I would track my heart rate using my Fitbit – not consciously, it would just be something I would notice days later. My heart, while playing roulette or slots or watching football, was beating like I'd been for a 2-mile run. And a 2-mile run was the last thing I wanted to do. Gambling came first.

The stresses of gambling addiction began to overtake any happiness I got from it. I was almost resigned to losing but carried on. I think this feeling is right at the heart of addiction. Knowing what you're doing is wrong but not being able to stop. I would have been happy if I couldn't gamble but something compelled me to carry on.

Gambling would always affect events that I was meant to be attending. I was never ready for anything as I was too busy gambling. A mate would come to pick me up and I'd keep him waiting while I was sat on my laptop gambling. 'Sorry mate, I was late getting in the shower,' I'd say. I'd also plan things which I'd then have to cancel due to having no money. A trip to the cinema or pub wouldn't be possible. I would also quite often choose gambling before sleeping which would lead to further complications with work and social events. The number of days I've spent working on empty – I'm sure I only got through my job because I was experienced and could work on auto pilot most of the time. Weekends would be spent drinking alcohol or laid in bed gambling and catching up on sleep.

At my worst, I really suffered from a lack of sleep. I would spend hours awake, gambling. I couldn't stop, I would mostly play all night until I had lost all my money. I would often get ill from being so run down due to a lack of sleep. The lack of sleep got to the point where it felt dangerous for my mental and physical health.

Gambling to the Experts

Compulsive gambling. Problem gambling. Pathological gambling. Addictive gambling. It has many names, all of which relate to the same problem. Lots of names, I think, partly due to the relatively little that is known about gambling addiction compared to other addictions. Is it taken seriously? I think it is being taken a lot more seriously nowadays but there is still a way to go for it to be recognised as it should. It will probably always be looked upon as being a problem that people don't want to talk about. A dirty secret for many suffering with it and easy to keep hidden most of the time with few tell-tale signs of a gambler and their addiction. It's easy for people to view other abuses, like alcoholism or drugs, as being uncontrollable whereas gambling is a choice. People may see it as an addiction for idiots or losers. I wanted to do more research into this as I fully believe once I was in the grip of the addiction, I felt there was nothing I could do but feed my urges.

What do the experts think problem gambling is?

Under the Diagnostic and Statistical Manual of Mental Disorders, Fifth Edition (2013) (American Psychiatric Association), gambling is now recognised as an addictive disorder, with sufferers exhibiting many similarities with those that suffer substance addictions. This highlights the relative infancy that research into gambling is at. During my 12 years of gambling, the problem has been reclassified as an addictive disorder rather than an impulsive disorder.

I feel like addiction is the most appropriate way to describe gambling. There must be more to it than just acting on impulse. Gambling, like many substance addictions, works on the brain's reward mechanisms.

Substance disorders have the following criteria:

- Increasing frequency and amount
- Increasing time spent
- Continuing use despite negative consequences
- Relationship problems
- Neglecting major roles and responsibilities
- Failed attempts to cut down or quit
- Loss of interest in enjoyable activities
- Preoccupations
- Compulsion

I have experienced every one of these while gambling.

Comparisons with substance addictions also ring a bell from a particular area of gambling. FOBT (fixed odds betting terminals in bookies shops) were once known as the 'crack cocaine of the betting industry' – a nickname coined specifically due to their drug-like addictive nature. At their height, these terminals which had roulette and slots games on allowed max bets of £100 every 20 seconds – this has thankfully been reduced to £2 in April 2019 due to new legislation. I'm not sure whether this was to combat gambling or the increased amount of money laundering that was happening through these machines. This is the same with restrictions on amounts that are deposited online. Proof is needed of funds – is this checking affordability for each player or for money laundering check purposes? I once used a loan for gambling and sent the document to the gambling site as evidence and they were fine with this as proof of funds, even though it clearly highlighted my gambling wasn't affordable. I understand it was me who gambled this money away, but I also feel I was vulnerable due to my addiction and this lack of control by the gambling site was neglectful. It's like buying a pint for an alcoholic, enabling the addiction with no moral thought.

Factors leading to gambling addiction are widely regarded as:

- Mental health disorders i.e. the presence of substance abuse problems, personality disorders, emotional states
- Ages and sex – gambling issues are mostly found in young and middle-aged men
- Impact of family or friends
- Personality traits
- Drugs with adverse side effects – e.g. antipsychotic medications or dopamine agonists

Other studies suggest:

- Traumatic conditions
- Job-related stress
- Solitude
- Other addictions

Lasting problems from this include relationship issues, serious money problems, legal issues including imprisonment, health problems and suicide including suicidal thoughts and attempts.

The dangerous problems that arise from gambling are what led to suicidal thoughts for me. Relationship issues, money problems and health problems all caused me to consider suicide.

Swedish research, if applied to the UK, suggests that 550 suicides a year in the UK are linked to gambling. People with gambling problems are 15 times more likely to take their own life. It's difficult to hear this and I feel for any families that have been through this.

Writing this chapter has surprised me and some of these facts are shocking. Something which seems so trivial and innocent to so many is actually killing people. People who see suicide as the only way out for them. Things such as smoking are not advertised due to the adverse side effects to health and yet gambling is one of the most widely advertised things on tv / radio / billboards. So many celebrities will put their face to this advertising without a second thought. And it's not just suicides – how many will suffer with mental health issues resulting from gambling?

Facts and Figures

As part of my research for this book, I have been looking at information presented by the National Audit Office from their analysis of Gambling Commission data. I was interested to see the growth of the gambling industry over the years that I had lived with the addiction. I could certainly feel the industry growing. The increase in betting companies online was just one of those signs. Also, the number of gambling-related issues in the news seems to have increased. I have read stories of addicts committing suicide, stealing to fund gambling debts and stories of people losing tens of thousands of pounds with relative ease. I wonder how many were like me though, suffering in silence.

The following facts show us the increased activity in gambling over the ten years to 2018–19:

Licensed gambling in Britain grew by 57 per cent or £4.1 billion in real terms in the ten years to 2018–19.

The total gross gambling yield (excluding the National Lottery) earned by gambling operators in Great Britain in 2018–19 was £11.3 billion. Gross gambling yield is the amount retained by operators after the payment of winnings, but before the deduction of costs of operation, according to the Gambling Commission, which regulates gambling in Britain.

The surge in licensed gambling was largely due to the rise in online gambling and mobile gambling. Operators' yield from licensed online gambling rose from £1 billion to £5.3 billion in the 10 years to 2019 according to the National Audit Office – that certainly isn't just reflecting an inflationary increase, but rather a booming growth in the gambling industry.

Online gambling is convenient and simple to get started with. It's also dangerous due to the lack of restrictions on both money that is put in to gamble with (personal loans for example) and the amounts that can be gambled. The £2 FOBT limit doesn't exist online. It's also a 24-hour-a-day activity and can be done in the comfort and secrecy of your own home.

The global, legal gambling market was estimated to be $335 billion in 2009. Extraordinary numbers.

Gambling On Everything

I have already spoken briefly about the diversity of things I would bet on. Whatever event or game there was for me to gamble on, I would gamble on it. It doesn't matter how complicated a game is, gambling on it is servicing a basic need. A need that can be fulfilled with something as simple as betting on heads or tails. If it provided me with the same 'high', I was happy. From Gambling Commission statistics, for the period April 2018 to March 2019, we can see the generated revenue by sector:

Sector	Generated revenue
Online	£5.36bn
Betting	£3.25bn
National Lottery	£3.01bn
Casinos	£1.18bn
Bingo	£0.68bn
Other lotteries	£0.51bn
Arcade	£0.43bn

I gambled on every one of these areas over the 12-year period that I gambled heavily. As with the above statistics, online gambling and sports betting amounted to the majority of my gambling. I would gamble mainly on the following:

Roulette

Roulette is a casino game I would regularly play, named after the French word meaning little wheel. In the game, players may choose to place bets on either a single number, various groupings of numbers, the colours red or black, whether the number is odd or even, or if the numbers are high (19–36) or low (1–18).

The problems I had, and many people have, is that this is a game of chance that would be played to win. Doesn't make sense, right? People will tell you there is strategy to win but it's not true. The house edge will see you lose. This is probably the game that I have lost most of my money on due to the opportunity for big bets. I have many times bet thousands of pounds on one spin of the wheel. The adrenaline rush was exhilarating.

Slots

Another game of chance, spinning wheels at up to £100 a spin, complete with bonus rounds. I have spent a lot of hours spinning these into debt for myself, waiting to hit that big jackpot. My biggest win was £13k from a £5 bet – this is not a brag; the money was eventually gambled away.

The variety of slots available is astounding. I had a look at one of the biggest bookmakers in the UK, and it has nearly 500 slots available to gamble on. Slots have a built-in RTP % which tells us what the % return to player is. This is usually 80–90%. This means for every £1 put in, the player's expected return is around 80–90p. Continued play on slots will always bring about a loss eventually and I was playing these a lot.

Football

Most of my sports betting was on football due to my interest in it and the fact I would watch a lot of games live anyway.

I could sub-divide this betting into an endless number of sub-categories – betting on goals, corners, double chance, correct score, goal scorers, draw no bet, cards… and many more. I was usually betting on over/under goals. This involves predicting the number of goals in a match. There is nothing you can do to correctly predict this. Stats and 'gut feelings' can only take you so far. You may feel in control, but it is factually unpredictable. Anyone that says otherwise is lying to you and probably themselves.

I would often go and watch my local team and have a bet on the match or be too busy watching my phone throughout the match checking scores from the other games happening at the same time.

Other Sports

Over the years, I have bet on everything from women's volleyball to men's badminton. If it was a sport that I could bet on, then I would. I didn't care if I didn't have the knowledge to support my bets, it was still chasing a gambling high and it sufficed for that. Tiddlywinks in Kazakhstan? If it exists, I'll have £50 on the team in red…

Horse Racing

Not something I was particularly interested in, but I would do it for the buzz and attended the races through my job a few times. I had no knowledge of horse racing whatsoever. That excitement, as the horses head for the finish line with mine slightly ahead and then collecting cash winnings, was enough of a rush.

Dog Racing

I had trips with work on a Friday night to the dogs. As with the horse racing, a lot of alcohol was consumed. Alcohol and gambling do not mix. My knowledge was lacking as with the horse racing. When in doubt with animals racing, look for the best names. For example, horses named Hoof Hearted or Bunny Killer (apparently named after it trampled a load of rabbits to death in its field). Or simply pick the animal that had a shit before the race. Apparently, they're lighter and quicker.

National Lottery

Not something you'd think to spend a lot of money on; however, I remember a few months where I would end up blowing a lot on lottery tickets, looking for that big win – yes, chasing at odds of 45 million to one!? If you're not sure what this means? Basically, if I played the lottery 45 million times, probability tells us I'd be expected to win it once. Realistically, it's not going to happen, is it!? Being struck by lightning, attacked by a shark, dying in a plane crash and winning an Oscar are all shorter odds than winning the National Lottery. Buying a ticket and dying before the draw takes place is also more likely to happen. If that doesn't put you off, I don't know what will!

Stocks and Shares

An unusual thing to gamble on but I found I got the same buzz from buying and selling shares. I wasn't patient with it either and was throwing money down the drain, not doing proper research and investing in highly volatile businesses. It took me a while to realise this was just simply replacing the high I got from gambling on casino games and sports betting.

House Edge

All casino games have a house edge. The house average or house edge or house advantage (also called the expected value) is the amount the player loses relative for any bet made, on average. This means playing these games for a continued amount of time will always end with the casino winning.

The American mathematician Patrick Billingsley summed it up very well when he said that 'no betting system can convert a sub fair game into a profitable enterprise.'

With the casinos having an edge, I asked myself, what would a gambling establishment describe gambling as?

A business set up with guaranteed profits taken from customers, or 'suckers', due to the one-sided nature, or edge, held by the said business.

I imagine something along those lines.

One thing I would always like to think was that I had a strategy to profit from these games, whether it was a betting amount strategy or using my knowledge of football to make decisions. At the end of the day, this is just another gambler's fallacy. Strategy would often come down to me putting on a series of impulsive football accumulators while drunk and hoping Lady Luck was favouring me. Strategy disappears when you're desperate.

'No one who shares a delusion ever recognizes it as such.'
– SF

A Session

What was the average gambling session to me when at its worst? I want to give a complete picture of what it was like when I was sat in my room. What were my thoughts and feelings as I sat loading up my laptop?

It wasn't always an easy decision to start gambling. I could spend days leading up to it, thinking I shouldn't do it. A lot of the time, if I had it in my head, I was going to start at some point.

Firstly, I would need to find an online betting site that I'd not already signed up with. I'd usually set up an account, lose lots of money, then end up setting limits on the account after, to stop me from using that site in the future. This meant I would need a different account when I wanted to gamble again. If I'd given my parents my debit card to 'look after', I'd have to set up a gambling account that accepted PayPal – with PayPal, I didn't need my debit card details – only my account number and sort code. Once the account was set up, I was ready to gamble.

I start off with what I would call a 'sensible deposit' for gambling, say £200. Typically, this would be gambled on either slots or a sports bet. Most of the time this £200 wouldn't last long. In the later stages of my gambling problems, £200 was nothing to me. What started as a typical sport bet of £1 or a slot spin of 50p had gone to the next level and that £200 didn't go far at all. So that's £200 gone in minutes.

My next deposit is invariably more than the first, £500, £700, £1,000. I'm chasing my losses.

I have lost all control. There's no turning back at this point, it's all or nothing. I'm usually on roulette at this point, betting thousands a spin, chasing the money I've lost. This can go one of two ways; I may go on a winning streak and be thousands up. I may go the other way and lose all my money. Either way, I will eventually end up losing, either now or a few days or weeks down the line. I can never ever walk away. I have never walked away a winner; the money has always gone back into gambling.

Every spin of the roulette wheel is sickening. My heart is racing, I'm sweating. I know I shouldn't be doing it, but I can't resist. That is the addiction. If you win, the euphoria felt is not comparable to anything. The losses feel like dark times. I get angry at losing. *The roulette wheel is rigged*, I would think.

So, I've deposited thousands, lost it. I receive an email from the betting company – we need details of your income for proof of funds, and proof of identity. So, AFTER I have lost thousands and they have my money, they now want proof of funds. This is just another failure of the government, the Gambling Commission, whoever. They say it's for money laundering purposes but what good is checking that now after the casino has allowed me to gamble!?

I have to get copies of my driving licence, the bank card I've used to gamble – if I've used one – and a copy of my ‘proof of funds’. I must do this without anyone noticing. Once this is done and verified, I can continue to gamble. I now must think about how I can get more money to gamble. I can first use my overdraft, and then it’s loans I turn to. These are usually bank loans – I’ve never used the payday loans for this. I once had to get a bank loan to cover my expenditure for other things as I’d got a loan and spent it all on gambling.

This was a vicious circle which continued to happen consistently for many years. I would make promises to not go beyond my initial deposit but would ALWAYS break the promise. I have NEVER in my years of gambling walked away up. It seems strange to say that now, but I could never walk away. Whether it was over the space of a few hours, a few days or a few weeks, I would always end up losing.

This was the worst chapter to write. It’s reflecting on the times when I was in the furthest reaches of addiction. This was the time when I wasn’t thinking about anyone but myself. This was the time when I was throwing my life away. I had no respect for anything, I didn’t care about anything.

Insanity: doing the same thing over and over again and expecting different results.

Did You Know?

I googled ‘mental health gambling’ and the second search result, at the time of writing this, is an advertisement for a gambling website and bonus offer! We don’t stand a chance…

I decided to do some more googling on my phone…

Search for 'Gambling Feelings'

A search for 'gambling feelings' brought up a lot of articles on problem gambling. More 'related' results below this include 'can gambling make you rich?', 'how do I win a bet every time?', 'do gamblers ever win?'. Unsurprisingly, the link to the 'can gambling make you rich?' is an article which says 'yes, there are ways gambling can make you rich.' At the foot of the page is a list of 'gambling organisations' including Gamblers Anonymous, GamCare and... Bet365, a well-known bookmaker. The ads on the page are for Foxy Bingo.

Search for 'Gambling'

A straight-up search for gambling is mainly a list of advertisements for well-known gambling websites. The news articles are about problem gambling – one story about a bloke who stole £300k to fund his gambling. Again, several articles and websites for problem gambling.

Search for 'How to Make Money?'

One advert relating to an online gambling company.

It seems whatever is typed in relating to gambling, there will be an advertisement for doing it from one of the hundreds of online bookmakers.

Google's Autocomplete

Gambling… addiction
Gambling… sites
Gambling… commission
Gambling… addiction help
Gambling… games
Gambling… help
Gambling… sites UK

Gambling is… bad
Gambling is… not a sin
Gambling is… a sin
Gambling is… killing me
Gambling is… a disease
Gambling is… a mugs game
Gambling is… ruining me

Gamblers are… losers
Gamblers are… addicted to losing
Gamblers are… stupid
Gamblers are… liars
Gamblers are… selfish
Gamblers are… like toilets
Gamblers are… idiots

Casinos are… rigged
Casinos are… evil
Casinos are… depressing
Casinos are… boring

Casinos are… bad
Casinos are… scams
Casinos are… for losers

Temptation

When dealing with a gambling addiction, it seems like there is no chance of getting away from the temptation to gamble. Whether it's the endless betting advertisements on TV or the bookies that seem to be on every street corner, gambling is normalised in everyday life. Smoking has seen a massive decline since the ban on advertising. It is no longer seen as glamorous and is mostly seen now as a destructive and expensive addiction. Gambling still has that factor of being 'a way to make money, with no negative side effects'. It's seen as a 'fun pastime which everyone should be involved in'. And it's this which fuels the industry and addiction.

It is estimated that £1.5 billion a year is contributed to the football industry from betting companies. In 2019, major bookies signed up for a 'whistle to whistle' ban on live sports advertising – i.e., no advertising five minutes before and after an event. However, this is still an issue and there is still no shortage of advertisements in stadiums, on football shirts and on the television. We live in a day and age now where advertising can be perfectly geared towards people.

On one occasion, my mum had said she had been googling on her iPhone some suggestions to help me stop gambling. She said, since doing this, she has been inundated with gambling advertisements for free spins and bonus offers from casino websites! It's crazy!

In terms of access to gambling, I decided to look at the quantity and concentration of bookies around my local area. Bear in mind I live in a little village which is around 10 miles from four different towns/cities.

5 Miles

One small independent bookmaker in the next village to mine.

10 Miles

An additional 39+ bookmakers and casinos. Increase the radius to 10 miles and straight away I have a ridiculous number of bookmakers and casinos to hand. I can see from the map that this doesn't even include all bookmakers – I should know, I visited them. I can see streets with 2+ bookmakers on them. I can see more than one of the same company in the same town centre.

30 Miles

An additional 30+ bookmakers and casinos. This is not including the villages surrounding the major towns and cities.

It does seem in the local towns that you can't walk more than five minutes without passing a bookmaker or casino. This shows that the demand for these establishments is there. They are generating enough income from customers to remain open, even after the new restrictions placed on the fixed odds betting terminals. One customer stated that after these restrictions were put in place, he would simply spend longer gambling. People who don't realise they have a problem will find it impossible to stop. More needs to be done to educate these people about how dangerous gambling is and how to be able to stop, rather than it just being so accessible and widely advertised. It doesn't feel like gambling is a choice anymore. Where is the moral consideration that would surely change this?

Gambling With Work

There were often instances when my work life and secret gambling life collided. Each year, my employer would pay for us to attend the horse racing in York or Chester. A couple of times, I was too tempted to say no, partly due to the fact it was a free day out, even though I knew it would have a negative impact on me. Gambling and alcohol – there was only going to be one outcome.

I would make the excuse that if I were in front of other people, especially work colleagues, I would be able to control my urges. I would take a set amount of cash and only use that. The truth is, it was all setting me up for a fall. Making excuses for my gambling became something I could do effortlessly.

The day would start at the pub with a pint and breakfast, before a coach journey to the racecourse, again with drinks. More drinking on arrival and I was never going to be in a fit state to make sensible decisions.

Even when I came away from the horses with money in my pocket, the gambling urge was in place. The next day, I would be thinking about gambling and inevitably this would lead to more gambling.

This was the same when I attended the dog racing with work. I would let myself go but eventually I would end up drunk and heading to the casino next door to the dog track.

In my last few years working for this employer, I managed to abstain from going to any gambling events – this was the easiest way to stop it causing further issues.

There were also the lower risk betting events that I was always torn as to whether I should take part or not. The sort of events that a lot of people, even those with no interest in gambling, would get involved with. The Grand National sweepstake or the weekly lottery syndicate we did. Inevitably, if I was taking part, it made me start thinking about gambling. This clarified my belief that I had to abstain from all forms of gambling if I was going to make this work. If I thought it was wrong, it almost certainly was.

It also didn't help at work; the fact that most of the lads in the office were into gambling of some sorts, mainly football betting. It was talked about constantly and I also shared an office with a bloke who loved 'get rich quick' schemes such as taking advantage of the cryptocurrency market. After the major slump in this market in 2018/19, I'm glad this was one of the few things I stayed clear of. Just being in environments like this aren't good and I had to learn techniques to deal with them – things such as being able to walk away from these conversations or change the conversation entirely. I spent a lot of time at work walking away to make coffees or 'go to the toilet' just for a break from these conversations.

The Casino

The night before my visit to the casino – mecca for the dedicated gambler – I am too excited to sleep. I lie awake thinking of my plan for the trip; I picture hitting that big win and walking away with wads of cash. It never crosses my mind, however often it has happened in the past, how much money I would in fact be throwing away.

As I lie in bed, insomnia hanging over me, I sit on my laptop watching videos of 'big wins in Las Vegas', or look at a website which offers a 'fool proof' strategy for winning at the roulette table. Deep down, I know this is all false glamorising of gambling and would in no way reflect my visit to the casino tomorrow.

The casino is seen as the more glamorous location to gamble, compared to being at the local bookmakers or sat alone at home – in truth, the bookies is probably more reflective of gambling, with the depressive atmosphere and faceless, agitated gamblers. Films such as 'Casino Royale' and 'Ocean's Eleven' show off the attractive side of gambling, the guys dressed in smart tux, fancy cocktails, winning money! Less well-known films such as 'Owning Mahowny' and 'The Gambler' reflect a more accurate side to gambling. The raw obsession and lengths people will go to due to gambling addiction.

It's the day of my trip and I park up in one of the endless empty spaces just outside the casino. I am excited. Destiny is calling me. I enter the grey, bleak building and show my membership card at the front desk. The décor inside of the establishment is anything but grey and bleak. Garish interior, flashing lights, excitable sounds. The woman on reception smiles and greets me and tells me to go on through. I feel like a kid being unleashed upon the playground at lunchtime. The endless possibilities and fun to be had. This is where I am meant to be, this is my calling in life, there is no other feeling like it. A rush of excitement and adrenaline courses through me. I would love to run around the place with a smile on my face. Of course, in reality I keep an icy exterior – I don't want people to know I'm a gambling addict.

Straight down to business, I'm here to make some money. I walk past the roulette tables, abuzz with people having fun. Glamorous croupiers raking up chips as an *unlucky* punter hits another loss on the roulette wheel. A cheer every now and again as a small group of people, who I assume aren't casino regulars but here for a fun day out, win on a slot machine. They're dressed up in fancy clothes, in contrast to my jeans, t shirt, jacket and trainers. I walk past the slot machines, all lit up like Blackpool Illuminations, each one playing a joyful tune. The lights attract people like moths to a flame. My heart is racing, and, for a gambler, this is the height of excitement. To just be there and ready to gamble is bliss.

Away from the hustle and bustle of the main tables and the slot machines, I spot the video roulette screens. I don't want to be disturbed and I head for a quiet seat in the corner – or more likely I feel ashamed and don't want to be in front of others while I lose money. I might as well have stayed at home, gambling on my laptop. However, there's just something about the casino which draws me in.

There are rows upon rows of electronic screens with little red leather bar stools in front of each one. A little side table for drinks. A button to call over a server. But I'm not interested in a drink right at this moment. I'm here to gamble.

I pull out my wallet, bursting with five, ten and twenty-pound notes I have drawn out from the cash machine outside the casino. I'm ready to play. Hopefully, this wad of cash will be three, four or maybe five times the size when I'm finished. I select a roulette table to play on – they have live footage of all the main tables and one automated wheel in front of the video screens – and I enter some cash. I start off small, maybe pull a twenty from my wallet and feed it into the greedy mouth of the machine which sucks it in willingly. I will never forget the sound this makes. I'm not sure why I only put £20 in, the damage is going to always be more than this. I stuff my wallet back in my pocket – again, why bother? The balance on the screen updates. I'm a tad anxious at this point but then remember, I could win loads of cash here and walk away a winner. The betting starts off low and controlled.

At this point, Keanu Reeves could ride past on a camel and I wouldn't look up from the roulette screen. I am so absorbed in the gambling, the wheel sucking me in like a black hole in space. They say even time is sucked into a black hole and for me sat in the casino, it flies by as well; hours would literally feel like minutes. Externally, I try to play it cool but inside I'm praying to the gambling gods. Is this even entertainment whatsoever for me at this point? Is this just me getting the high that my brain craves?

I start off well and in no time I'm £200 up. I start to relax. Good times. Heart racing still. I get an alcoholic drink to calm me down and tip the server fifty pence. *Damn, it feels good to be a gangsta.* As I relax, my bets get higher and higher, looser and looser. I move over to the slots. Different game, same buzz. I hit a bonus – £400 up. *Right, go and cash out,* I tell myself. I go and cash out. It's a long walk to the cage. They're usually at the back of the casino. They say it's to put off any possible burglary attempts. I say that it's because it causes anyone withdrawing cash to have further to walk when they've won, and with that, more chance of them putting their money back in.

I go to the toilet (bear with me, this is an important observation). I've never really thought about the toilets in a casino before but what do they always have in common? They're bloody luxury. And it confirms what all gamblers know but choose to ignore – casinos aren't built on customers winning. The only winners are the casino – and some of this money is spent on lovely places for the customers to piss. After all, a comfortable gambler is an active gambler.

I walk back over to the machines, apparently not happy with a £400 win. Or I just want that buzz again. I bet small; I'm only doing it to get a hit. I use the Martingale system – it's risky but I've used it in the past and it worked well (I put aside in my mind the number of times it hasn't worked for me). This system works by doubling my bet each time I lose – when it eventually wins, I'll be in profit. Three reds have landed on roulette, so I bet black with £20. It hits red again. This time I bet £40 on black. Red again. This time I bet £80 on black. Its green, zero. No win. I have my final bunch of cash and decide to place it all on black, all my eggs in one basket, one amazing adrenaline rush – it must be black now. I see the ball landing; my heart is racing but I try to remain cool in public. I see the ball nestled in 3, red. My heart sinks. I call it ridiculous. I'm not sure how a ball moving 'round a wheel is anything but random, but I call it ridiculous. Blame it on magnets. Unfair. *How have I just lost £400 in a matter of minutes?* Disbelief soon disappears and I begin to decide how I will get my money back. Not a good decision, especially after starting drinking. Alcohol has lowered my inhibitions; I think nothing of chasing my losses.

Winning and losing isn't important to a gambler. The addiction is to the high, and this comes with both winning and losing. Winning just enables more gambling and losing brings about negative consequences afterwards.

I check every nook and cranny of my wallet for any more cash to gamble with. There isn't any. I head to the cash machine – *£1.50 for a withdrawal* it says. I shake my head, *how extortionate*! An observation by Casanova, who had a side-line in gambling, who noted that inside every serious gambler lurks a miser. I can see this. The greed to want that free money is massive but on the other hand, a £1.50 fee for withdrawing money is seen as ridiculous, even when I've just lost a load of money.

Fuck it, I make the withdrawal. Turns out both me and the casino are as greedy as one another. One of the worst feelings is when you're in deep, lost loads of money, but keep gambling to try and win, even though you know you should walk away. A further £300 is taken in a matter of moments. There isn't a penny left to gamble with. I sit there almost shaking, empty inside. I look up from the machine and blink, my eyes readjusting to the room that hasn't been there for the last 30 minutes. I take a few final sips of my drink. *What time is it?* I have no idea. That's another casino trick. No clocks, no windows. If someone loses track of time, they're more likely to continue gambling.

Not me. I have no money left. One more toilet trip in the grand bathroom, a wash of the hands with the Molten Brown soap, a look in the mirror at myself in disgust, and then I'm gone.

The disgust I must shake quickly, I must go back to living behind my mask.

Boy, what I'd do to get that fifty pence tip back from the server.

Casino Tricks

I have mentioned previously about the tricks used by casinos to keep people gambling. Here is a list of the top 10. Apparently, anything is acceptable when money is involved. Apart from fairness and morality – that goes out of the window.

1. **No clocks / no windows** – a great trick employed by the casino to hide the passage of time. The number of times I've left a casino and been surprised at the time or the daylight/moonlight outside. It's very unnerving.
2. **A sense of control** – casinos love to make you think you have some sort of control over events, even though they are heavily favoured towards the house. Rolling the dice in craps or being able to make a choice in blackjack – these are both examples of false control.

3. **Free drinks, notably alcohol** – a perk of being a player? Any gambler will tell you that alcohol and gambling are a dangerous mix. It relaxes and can cause questionable decision making. Also, free coffees and coke – great for keeping players alert and gambling.
4. **Lights, lights and more lights** – often accompanied with loud music – another way of keeping the interest of a casino goer, attracting people to gamble more. Again, lights and sounds keep people alert and playing.
5. **A maze of machines and tables** – strategically placed everywhere. Need the toilet? Have a gamble on the way. Want to get food and drink? Play a slot first. Want to take your winnings home? Walk past hundreds of gambling machines before you can get away.
6. **Near wins** – they keep the player interested. That jackpot could be just around the corner. You think you were so close to winning when you got three jackpot symbols in a row, when in reality it's simply an illusion.
7. **Luxury facilities** – feel like a king. It makes the casino seem like one big luxury club with you as a member. What a lovely place to go to the bathroom.
8. **Free bonuses and perks for loyal players** – it keeps attracting the gamblers.
9. **Garish colours** – everywhere! Quite an amusing one; the garish carpets and wallpaper are designed this way as it is believed it keeps player alert and awake. It probably has science to it as the majority of casinos

look like they copied their décor direct from a 1970s' house.

10. **Free oxygen for everyone!?** – I'm not so sure I believe this one, but it certainly makes scientific sense. Oxygen could be pumped into the casino to keep players alert and awake – I wouldn't put anything past them to be honest!

I believed walking into these places that I would win every time – no matter how many times the opposite happened. With these things going on, who stands a chance of winning? All this plus the house edge in all games, it's ridiculous to think casinos attract anyone apart from the one-off nights out which are purely for fun. I don't think these people are the casino's main customers though. It was me. Using the place for a buzz. An expensive and destructive high.

Merry Christmas and a Happy New Bank Loan

Christmas is meant to be a joyous time of year, but for me, it was one of the hardest. In general, it can be a difficult time for people, whether they have mental health issues or not. We can sit and contemplate a year of missed opportunities or pine for people we have lost, people we would usually spend this time of year with.

I'm not sure whether I inexplicably saw gambling as means to make money during an expensive time of year, or whether I saw it as a distraction from other issues. One thing is clear. I would always be in deep shit by the end of the holiday period, in much more debt than when I came into it.

I recall one such occasion in particular. 'Twas the night before our annual Christmas party with work and I was awake all-night watching basketball. I'm not sure whether I enjoyed watching basketball or it was just the buzz from gambling on it. Let's just say nowadays I have a lot of knowledge on a sport which I rarely get chance to watch – who wants to stay up until all hours watching a sport they're not gambling on, eh!? I was gambling that night on college basketball, my knowledge of which didn't go beyond being able to spell the team names (unless those teams were Mississippi, Tennessee or Massachusetts!!). I had waited up until around 5am to see my bet come in. Most of my bets on basketball revolved around total points scored, I guess because of my affinity to totals goals betting on the football in the UK. Brilliant, my bet had come in and I had some extra cash for my work do. Wait a second, that sounds too good to be true, right? Within ten minutes of winning the money, which I'd waited up all night to collect, I had lost it again in the online casino. The money frittered away in seconds on roulette.

To say it tore me up is an understatement. I was now heading out on my annual Christmas do to get pissed having had two hours asleep. Alcohol would now replace the gambling fix for the next day.

Betting on amateur basketball, for which I had no knowledge, proved to myself that gambling for me was never about winning and losing, black and white. I would gamble on anything to get the buzz. Christmas day would find me betting on football going ahead in non-Christian countries. Was I an expert in Egyptian football? Not by a long stretch, but it was just another way to get my fix. The Christmas and New Year period has lots of English football to bet on too. It was always a time when I would lose lots of money.

Merry fuckin' Christmas.

That Big Win

Ask many gamblers why they do it and common answers will be that they are looking for that one big win or want to make a living from professional gambling. For a start, both are very unlikely. But it is still something I would be considering while playing.

If I win £50k, I'll stop gambling forever. If I win back all the money I've lost over the years, I'll stop. Truth is, I don't know how much money I've lost over the years. This was just a line I would tell myself to justify carrying on. I know 100%, no doubt, that if I had won a large sum, I would have carried on gambling until it was all gone. I've had big wins, as high as £16k, on several occasions and nothing changed. I would ALWAYS gamble the money away in the end.

I've heard people say 'buy something with your winnings' if you hit a large sum. It's, again, people trying to justify gambling. The money is always recycled back into the gambling machine.

Making a living from gambling was another pipe dream I held as a gambler. If I could control myself and use my knowledge of sports, I could make a monthly wage from gambling. Of course, winning isn't guaranteed, and control certainly isn't guaranteed on my part. There is always that person inside who will end up gambling it all away.

Another thing a problem gambler will see as a necessity is hitting rock bottom. Hit rock bottom and then it's time to seek help. Rock bottom for me is endless. Rock bottom and then some. Every time I gambled, I ended up lower than the time before. What was I waiting for? Where could my addiction have led as I chased an ever-diminishing high. A time when it got so bad that my suicidal thoughts would become a reality? Go as far as stealing money to fund my addiction? There is no waiting for rock bottom – change it now so you'll never be at the bottom again.

Beaten the Addiction?

There were many times when I thought I had beaten my gambling addiction but, in fact, I was feeding it in other ways. A classic case of this was when I started to invest in stocks and shares. A reasonable way to invest money to some. Another way of gambling large amounts of money to access the thrill for me. I opened a stocks and shares ISA with my bank and began investing in 'penny stocks'. These are smaller companies with lower share values – they present higher risk but also higher reward. What started as investing small amounts soon led to thousands of pounds being thrown away. I was doing little research into it – again, it wasn't about winning and losing – it was about the excitement of the rollercoaster.

The National Lottery was another example of this. I wasn't playing it like most 'normal' folk. I was buying hundreds of tickets a month, expecting to win big. It was that thought of 'if I win big, I can pay off my debts and walk away'. In hindsight, without help, I know I would have carried on gambling even if I did win big. Winning wouldn't have helped. The very last time I gambled, I was in profit by around £20,000. A big £13,000 single win on a slot machine on a Sunday afternoon. Where is that money now? It's certainly not in my pocket!

Gamblers Anonymous? Yes, Please!

Someone once suggested Gamblers Anonymous (GA) to curb my gambling. There are meetings all around the UK where gamblers can go and meet with other gamblers to discuss their personal experiences of addiction. There was one in my local town that a work colleague of mine went to. For me, GA didn't feel like an option though. The thought of going to a therapist or my friends and revealing my addiction was tough enough. Going and revealing it to ten or twelve other random people would have been too hard for me at that time. I was struggling with anxiety in public as it was. The bottom line is, I was a gambler, and happy being anonymous.

I can see the benefits of GA. Talking to people about addiction is without doubt one of the best things that you can do.

I remember the first few times I sat down with individual friends and revealed my addiction. It took so much to tell them, and I would break down in tears as I did. It would bring up all the feelings that had been building. The shame, the loss. But this was many years ago and I continued to gamble even after telling people. Sharing my secrets was relieving me of nothing, I was completely lost.

Alcohol

Gamble. Drink. Gamble. Drink. Gamble. Drink. Gamble. Drink.

Gambling and alcohol. A vicious unhealthy cycle for me. I would turn to alcohol to forget about the destruction I was causing myself with gambling. I was binge drinking a lot on the weekend and even going out in the week and heavily drinking. It is said that one addiction can often be replaced by another. I wouldn't say my drinking got to the point of true addiction, I was more of a binge alcoholic at times, but the way I used it as to self-medicate in between big gambling losses wasn't healthy for my mind or body. Alcohol is good for relieving anxieties in the short term, useful at helping to forget. But it's a short-term solution to a bigger issue. I would always wake up the next day and, unsurprisingly, my problems hadn't disappeared but now seemed to be magnified.

The link between gambling and drinking is something which I think a lot of other gamblers can relate to. Even casinos know the relationship and offer free alcohol to keep people in their casinos gambling. Gamblers show less control when drinking due to the effects of alcohol consumption. It relaxes and takes away any fear when gambling. Often, I would find myself returning from a night out at the pub and loading up my laptop to gamble. Not only does it relax, it also affects judgement and I would usually lose a lot of money when under the influence of alcohol. I would then wake up feeling like absolute shit and my anxieties were a hundred times worse.

Both gambling and alcohol habits are destructive when pastime becomes addiction. The mix of both is a lethal cocktail.

Anything Is Better Than Lies and Deceit

The harshest part of gambling when I look back must be the continuous lying and deceit. After a while, my family knew I had a gambling problem, and this was mainly due to the fact I would go to them for money when I had none. I would constantly, time after time after time, make the promise I wouldn't continue to gamble. Even though I did want to give up, the grip it firmly had on me meant I would stop for a while but would soon start up again. A lot of the time I believed myself when I said I wouldn't gamble with money from my parents. However, most of the time, I did end up gambling. It was a sudden switch from wanting to get better for me and my family, to being sat alone and not being able to stop the urge.

I feel so lucky to have always had the support of family and friends. They have had to deal with the lies and deceit first-hand. But they have always stood by me. It would be a whole other book for someone else to write about the other side of gambling and how it affects the friends and family of a gambler.

However much I spoke about changing and starting again, I would always go back to gambling when life got a bit difficult or when I thought I could make some extra cash. And with any amount of measures in place to stop myself from gambling, a gambler will ALWAYS find a way around them. And it's not just from my experiences. I have witnessed first-hand other gamblers coming up with the same lies.

Even today, only a handful of people know the extent of my problems. I have always been very secretive, even to my closest friends, about my gambling. They knew I liked to gamble but would be shocked to what extent. Never judge a book by its cover.

I had never been the sort of person to enter a bookmaker's. This was a dirty little secret; I wasn't about to go and show my true colours in front of other people. I was embarrassed. Ashamed.

I started to go to the casino near my work with a friend from work. This would turn into another outlet for me to lose money. This also opened my eyes to how popular these places were with people, a lot I could see were far too into it for it to be called a hobby.

Lies

'Being entirely honest with oneself is a good exercise.'

– SF

I was prepared to tell many lies throughout my gambling problems. These were told so I could carry on with my addiction. I was desperate. I told them to myself and to the people around me. Lies such as:

1. **I don't have a gambling problem** – for a long time, I would insist I didn't have any problems with gambling, even though I was ticking a lot of the boxes for a problem gambler.
2. **I can stop gambling at any time** – again, early on, I did believe I had control of my gambling when it was already controlling me.
3. **I'm not affecting anyone else** – I would often think it was only about me and my feelings when it was also affecting everyone around me.
4. **I haven't gambled** – a lie I would tell all the time. I would hide my gambling activities even though my mood swings would give it away.
5. **I can be trusted with money** – the number of times I said I could be trusted with money but was planning on gambling straight away when I got chance.
6. **I can be trusted** – trust is a hard thing to earn. I won't have it until I've earned it
7. **I'll never gamble again** – said time and time again. The proof as they say, is in the pudding.

It's an awful world of lies and deceit that is created. I was blind to it most of the time and would only realise what was happening when I was outside of my bubble. I'm not a person that lies about everything but when it came to gambling, I would do anything to carry on getting my fix.

I even wondered if this honour to keeping my secrets had affected me more deeply than just with the gambling. That sense that things should be covered up, almost hiding myself behind a barrier. Do I unknowingly still have this barrier up? The only way to tell was to stop gambling.

Communication

I would suggest that good communication is everything when overcoming gambling issues. Whether it's just being able to talk to someone at any time about feelings, related to gambling or not, or calling up someone when an urge to gamble is occurring to take your mind off it.

It's something that takes A LOT of practice. I'm still getting used to it now and have recently been guilty of not pushing myself to do it. I'm a bit of an introvert and always found it easy to keep everything to myself rather than talking to people.

I just try to be honest rather than lying to people that everything is fine.

TALK.

Gambling to You

I asked a few people who knew about my gambling addiction to describe gambling in five words.

'Scary, frightening, agonising, ugly, heart-breaking.'

'Evil, destructive, disease, addictive, tumour-like.'

'The gambling industry is sick.'

'Hurt, addiction, loss, destructive, consequences.'

'Fear, overwhelmed, anger, courageous, survive.'

'A big, massive, twat head.'

Credit

You might ask how someone can get in so much trouble with gambling debt. How was I funding my addiction once my salary wasn't enough to gamble with?

The truth is, I was using every available means to obtain credit to gamble with. It's not as hard as you'd imagine, simply down to the regulations which are lacking. Gambling companies are happy to take money without asking many questions. Their only concern is their bottom line. I didn't need to steal money, something I've read about a lot of gambling addicts resorting to. I would start with my own money in my bank account and once that had gone, I would go into my overdraft and use that to gamble with. It was so easy. Once that money had gone, I would use credit cards – some with £3,000 plus credit limits on them. This is an issue when it comes to gambling addiction and one that has been addressed recently to stop gamblers using credit cards to fuel the addiction. In April 2020, regulations were introduced to stop credit cards being used for gambling transactions. Sadly, those regulations were too late for me. I racked up massive credit card debt which attracted interest as well as transaction fees.

As I came to realise, gamblers will find any way possible to place their next bet. Regulations, in my mind, need to be more stringent and advances are only a fraction of what they need to be.

If you have a steady job and no major outgoings such as a mortgage, its relatively easy to obtain loans from banks and loan companies. I would say the loan was for 'other expenditure' and use it to gamble with. I am slowly paying these loans off and I thank God I'm not in debt to more unscrupulous characters.

There were times when my dad would pay money into my account to cover my debts and I would end up using this money to gamble with. It's fucking awful when I think about this now. Another time, I blocked gambling transactions on my bank card but bypassed this by using a PayPal account as the 'middleman' to move money into an online gambling account. I am ashamed of these actions, but I wanted to highlight the fact that there isn't much that will stop an addiction at its height.

Gambling created a vicious cycle for me and is probably the same story for many others. It got to the point where there was no difference between winning and losing. They were the same. And even if I did win, the money would be sat burning a hole in my pocket until I gambled again. Winning, losing, it didn't matter. Gambling was horrendous either way.

Breaking the Habit

As mentioned earlier, I had not talked to many people about my gambling problems. Talking to a professional therapist, trained in Cognitive Behavioural Therapy (CBT), was the first step I needed to make.

Talking to someone was like a weight being lifted from my shoulders.

CBT is an interesting concept which works to break the 'habit' of gambling by changing the way you think. Gambling became an automatic thought process for me. For example, if

I was feeling in a low mood, I would automatically turn to gambling. If I was struggling for cash during a month I would turn to gambling as a way to 'earn some extra cash'.

Throughout the CBT process, I was encouraged to keep a 'thought diary'. This was where I would write down any times where I thought about gambling and details about the thoughts. CBT is then about working to make more realistic expectations of these thoughts. For example, if I had the thought to gamble due to wanting more money, the realistic expectation here is that gambling isn't a way to make money. When have I ever 'made money' from gambling!?

Example of a basic thought diary completed for gambling addiction:

DATE: 01/01/2020

SITUATION – What situation was I in that made me think about gambling? Sat in the car and hear a sports betting advert offering a bonus for new joiners.

UNHELPFUL THOUGHT – What unhelpful thought occurred? I could take advantage of that bonus and place one bet.

FEELING – How did I feel? Nervous but excited. I want to gamble.

WHAT IS A MORE HELPFUL THOUGHT? – What is a more realistic thought? Don't gamble. When has it ever stopped at just one single bet?

OUTCOME – Don't gamble. Put on some music and move on.

CBT also explores the idea of 'riding the urge'. An urge can come, making me want to gamble, but this urge will peak at a certain point and eventually pass. Learning to 'ride' this urge will enable someone to decrease the time it takes for an urge to pass. Don't give in to the gambling urge straight away.

CBT showed me that not addressing my thoughts about gambling was going to cause me serious harm in the long term. It was described by my therapist as a bottle. As the bottled fills with water, it has nowhere else to go. As more and more water is added, the pressure builds. Eventually, this pressure becomes too much for the bottle to hold, and it explodes. Not addressing my thoughts was the same as the water in the bottle – it would eventually be too much for my brain to take and I would end up gambling. And gambling in an explosive manner.

> *'Unexpressed emotions will never die. They are buried alive and will come forth later in uglier ways.'*
>
> – *SF*

CBT taught me to own my addiction. I would often talk to my therapist but not speak of it as my addiction. She made me realise I needed to accept it was me. I have this problem. I am an addict. I must work towards stopping this.

CBT does work. It's something though which needs to be kept on top of. If you stop using the techniques above, the risk of going back to old habits is high. This was partly my problem. I struggled to keep up with using the techniques I had learned. Also, my issues went deeper, and it wasn't helping the addict inside me and the mental health issues I was beginning to harbour in a worse way than ever. Stopping gambling was beginning to affect me.

The big question I ask is, did CBT help break the addiction or just the habit? Can the addiction ever be broken? I think what I must realise is that if I gamble, it will serve the addiction, in the same way a beer will serve an alcoholic or heroin will serve a drug addict.

Unhelpful Thoughts

I began to realise what unhelpful thoughts I was having in relation to my gambling habits as well as my general mental health. Due to years of having these thoughts, they become automatic and this is when they're at their most dangerous. An example of these thoughts are as follows:

Mental Filtering

This is when we notice only what the filtering allows us to see. In gambling, an example is only remembering the wins and not the losses.

Prediction

Believing we know what will happen in the future. In gambling, it is a common misconception that we can predict the next number in roulette based on previous numbers which have come, for example. In football we believe we can predict future results based on past results.

In roulette, this is known as the gambler's fallacy. The flawed belief that if a particular event occurs more frequently than normal during the past, it is less likely to happen in the future (or vice versa), when it has otherwise been recognised that the probability of such events does not depend on what has happened in the past. The number of times I've *chased* a colour on roulette thinking *it must be due to come in.*

Mind-Reading

Assuming we know what others are thinking. This affected my mental state a lot, assuming people were judging me for the things I've done, even with people who didn't know I was a gambling addict.

Compare and Despair

Seeing only the good and positive aspects in others and getting upset when comparing ourselves negatively against them. I would succumb to this after losing a lot of money – look at everyone else buying cars and houses and I'm left with nothing.

'The only person you have to compare yourself is you in the past.'

– SF

Judgements

Making evaluations or judgements about events, ourselves, others, or the world, rather than describing what we actually see and have evidence for. A dangerous thought for a gambling addict with mental health issues.

Emotional Reasoning

I feel bad so it must be bad. I feel anxious so I must be in danger. This was particularly true once my anxieties set in due to the gambling.

Mountains and Molehills

Exaggerating the risk of danger or the negatives. Minimising the odds of how things are most likely to turn out or minimising the positives. Again, dangerous for a gambling addict and person with anxieties.

Catastrophising

Imagining and believing that the worst possible thing will happen. My severe anxieties had me thinking like this in a lot of situations.

Black and White Thinking

Believing that something or someone can be only good or bad, right or wrong, rather than anything in between or 'shades of grey'. I was very much a black and white thinker and had to change this.

Fact or Opinion

I remember receiving a small card during my CBT which had two simple columns on it – Fact and Opinion. This would become important for my mental health recovery. It read as follows:

Fact – evidence based, undisputed, driven by rational thought, head.

Opinion – based on belief or personal view, arguable, driven by emotion, heart.

It's an important thing to remember but easy to forget. Fact and opinion become blurred at times when in the gambling bubble, as well as in a lot of aspects of life. Also in CBT was the concept of the mind bully. It theorises we are in a constant battle in our heads. The key is, don't believe all you think. We should acknowledge these thoughts but shift focus. A very tricky concept to follow but something to be very mindful of.

Another idea I was given with regards to controlling gambling was to set a screensaver or wallpaper on my phone of something that gives me a reason not to gamble. Something that keeps me grounded, in the present, and doesn't allow me to be taken away and allow the gambler in me to come forward. At first, I was dubious of this but today I have screensavers and wallpapers of these things – for me it's my family, girlfriend and friends. It's important to stay outside of that bubble. To not be that addict.

CBT taught me it's important to be prepared for situations. Not preparing for situations where gambling may turn up is just asking for trouble. At the time of my CBT, this situation was a stag weekend I was going on. I knew there was a possibility that poker would be suggested or a trip to the casino. Both things which were common in this friendship group. It happened that in the end neither of these things happened, but it was important that I was prepared. What does prepared mean? I would only take so much cash with me, leave my debit card at home. I would be ready to not gamble, to say to people I didn't want to. To make sure I have access on my phone, to my thought diaries and my pictures that remind me why I don't gamble.

Delay. Distract. Decide

This is an effective strategy to curb gambling habits. The last barrier that CBT taught me to stop myself from gambling. It should become second nature, become the new habit that gambling once was.

Delay

I have a gambling thought. Can I delay gambling? Take some time. 10 seconds. 20 seconds. A minute. 2 minutes. 5 minutes. Just stop for as long as you can.

Distract

What can I do to distract myself? Make a cup of coffee. Take a walk. Talk to someone, not necessarily about gambling.

Decide

Why shouldn't I gamble? What are the disadvantages of gambling? Make the decision to not gamble.

At first, I was taking a lot of walks and making a lot of coffees, but at least I wasn't gambling.

Distract

There are many ways that I can distract myself when a gambling urge rears its ugly head. It's a particularly hard discipline to master. Especially, when I would spend hours alone with my laptop and the urge was always too much to resist. Before I knew it, I was signing up to a new gambling website.

Coffee. Football. Walk. Gym. Film. Friends. Family. Read. Sleep. Eat. Wash. Eat more. Run. Drive. Draw. Crossword.

Literally anything that you can do to distract yourself. Sitting and thinking about gambling is not going to help. It's not always easy to do certain things, like going for a run at 1am, but it's about finding anything that will help at any time. A lot of the time just talking to someone about absolutely any old shit helps a lot.

Sketching

One of my favourite ways to distract myself from any type of problem is sketching. It has always been an outlet for me and has also been a signal for my mental state. If I'm finding time to sketch, it usually means I am pretty happy and content with life.

Sketching is also an interesting outlet for emotions. I know that when I'm feeling pretty low, the kinds of drawings I do will differ from when I'm in a good mood. Just closing my eyes and deciding what to draw and more often than not it's my feelings that decide it. Darkness. Light. Anger. Happiness. Anxiety. Relaxation.

Being able to sit and sketch and be comfortable with your own thoughts is a sign that things are better. If they're not OK, and I want to forget thoughts, this is when I used gambling and alcohol to distract myself.

Physical Control

As well as breaking thought patterns and habits, there are physical controls which I like to implement when I'm possibly feeling unsteady. I used to think I had to rely on my own self-control but sometimes it's easier to just not put yourself under the stress and pressure of being able to gamble. By making it almost impossible.

A lot of the time, especially during the early months after a gambling lapse, it's much easier to have physical controls in place rather than just relying on other cognitive behavioural therapy techniques. These physical controls for me have included:

- Having someone in charge of my debit card.
- Having someone keep access to my bank account.
- Closing any gambling accounts, or putting restrictions on them.
- Closing my PayPal account.

I have learned that, in relation to some of these, this is not ideal most of the time but sometimes it's necessary and, most importantly, works. Yes, I feel like a toddler being told he can't have some sweets at the supermarket, but if it works to keep your head above the water, I say do it. Don't fear relying on these techniques. It would be ideal to have your bank card, but it's even more important to have money in your bank account. And to not be gambling.

Why Shouldn't I Gamble?

- Where will I be in ten years' time if I carry on gambling?
- Think about my family, friends and relationships and how they are suffering.
- Do I want independence, to be able to live on my own two feet?
- When I gamble, I can never quit and run. My debts are clearing, I don't want them any bigger.
- I want to protect my mental health for the future. The last time I gambled, I felt I could never face up to anything ever again. I wanted to curl up and disappear. Remember this feeling.
- I want my self-respect back.
- I want to be proud of something.
- I want to be able to help other people with similar problems.
- I want to have more money, to spend on things that make me happy.
- I want to focus 100% on a career.
- I know from experience, gambling does not make me happy in the end.

Mood Lifter

I came home from the pub five hours late last night.

"Where have you been?!" screamed my wife.

I said, "I've been playing poker with some mates."

"Playing poker with some mates?" she repeated. "Well, you can pack your bags and go!"

"So can you," I said. "This isn't our house anymore."

What's the difference between prayer in church and prayer in a casino? In a casino, you really mean it.

How do you make a small fortune gambling? Start with a large fortune.

A small man admitted himself into rehab for his gambling addiction. It's OK, he's a little better.

They say one out of every seven friends has a gambling addiction. My money's on John.

Part II – Mental Health

How Do I Feel?

A difficult question to answer.

Hopeless. What future do I have? Ashamed. Angry. Why have I lived my life like this? Suicidal. I don't want to be here anymore. Anxious. About everything.

Happy and content. Hopeful that I can change. Excited. About my prospects for the future.

Moods change. With mental illness, the lows feel as low as you could possibly go. The highs feel few and far between. My moods have over time, through hard work on my self-awareness, became manageable and balanced towards more positive than negative. And that's enough for me.

Mental Health

'The mind is like an iceberg; it floats with one-seventh of its bulk above water.'

– SF

It is only in the last couple of years that I started to become aware of my mental health and how it's been affected by my gambling past. I now have no doubt the impact on my mental health was significant. Gambling had become the crutch which I used to get through any situation. I was living in a bubble, the negative impacts building in the background, brewing like a volcano ready to erupt. The eventual eruption would have given Krakatoa a run for its money.

As I gambled less and less, my mental health issues came to the forefront. I had to take notice. It began at first with small signs of anxiety. This got worse and worse over time until it was crippling. This also eventually led to severe depression, anxieties' partner in crime.

As I was oblivious a lot of the time, I'd like people to become more aware of their mental health. It is so important and dangerous if it gets out of hand, as it did with me.

Early Life

I often think about my early life and consider if there was anything that would have been linked to the gambling and resulting depression that came after. In terms of mental health, I don't believe I had any big issues. I had anxieties, but I imagine a lot of young kids do. Mine were often extremely unfounded and usually related to medical hypochondria. I used to watch that '999' show with Michael Burke and it literally scared the shit out of me. I remember one episode which explained the symptoms of meningitis. It was describing the 'glass test' for *meningococcal septicaemia* – it could be used to see if a rash disappears when pressure is applied to the skin, by pressing the side of a clear glass against the skin. I'm not kidding when I say I spent weeks thinking I had rashes on my skin, checking them with a glass once I'd finished drinking out of it. I'm almost glad Google didn't exist back then; I'd be diagnosing myself with all sorts. *OK, I'm sure I have dengue fever.* I'm not even going to bother telling the story of the polystyrene ball that ended up stuck in my ear. We can just agree, yes, I had my anxieties.

It's funny to compare my problems now to those I had as a kid. It puts things into context. This is something I have become more aware of – taking the 'well, things could be a lot worse' approach to situations.

I think, overall, I had a happy childhood full of love and good fun. I ate my greens. I finished my entire chocolate advent calendar by the 3rd of December. Me and my sister put trowels in the tumble drier and turned it on, just because. As a toddler, I jumped headfirst into a window, who knows why. In terms of gambling, nothing springs to mind relating to that specifically.

Gambling addiction was long considered by the American Psychiatric Association to be an impulse control disorder rather than an addiction. Impulsivity is now seen as a common trait shared by problem gamblers. To act on impulse is 'actions that are poorly conceived, prematurely expressed, unduly risky, or inappropriate to the situation and that often result in undesirable outcomes.'

Was I impulsive before I started gambling? Not in dangerous way, but I was impulsive. Was I addicted to anything? Not really. I've always tended to go 'all in' when I have an interest in something. I'm quite an 'all or nothing person'. I either had a shaved head or long curly hair when younger, I either binged on alcohol or didn't drink at all. I've collected everything that is collected – coins, stamps, Pokémon cards, Pogs, Premier League sticker albums etc. It was just part of my nature when I was growing up. Does this have any sort of link to gambling? Pokémon came up with the most lucrative tag line of all time, 'Gotta catch 'em all.' Is it gambling collecting Pokémon cards? Maybe…

I remember as a kid I would love to go into the amusements at the seaside and throw a load of two pence pieces into the push machines. This was two pence at a time, but it was still about that buzz of maybe winning a crappy cheap toy. It wasn't about the toy; it was about just winning. The chance.

I'd see the ten or twenty pence ones and I'd think *Whoa, I could put some in there*. This is alike to my gambling. Always wanting to up the stakes, up the possible rewards.

Apart from this, I can't remember anything else which I would relate to gambling before I started putting on football accumulators when I was 18 years old.

There was a part of gambling which inherently played on my mild OCD (obsessive compulsive disorder). Choosing roulette numbers based on crazy coincidences, to the point where I became superstitious. I was trying to find order in randomness, a crazy and dangerous game. I would feel the need to carry on gambling, say, if I were £984 up, I would need to keep playing until I was up £1,000. I would chase losses as I couldn't bear to be walking away a loser. Compulsivity is similar but different to impulsivity. Compulsivity is 'a tendency to repeat the same, often purposeless acts, which are sometimes associated with undesirable consequences.' I look at my compulsivity now and think, *You idiot*.

Depression

What is depression? After having suffered and continuing to suffer from it, I can tell you I'm still not sure of the answer to this question. Medically speaking, depression (source: MedicineNet.com) is,

'An illness that involves the body, mood, and thoughts and that affects the way a person eats, sleeps, feels about himself or herself, and thinks about things. Depression is not the same as a blue mood. It is not a sign of personal weakness or a condition that can be wished away. People with depression cannot merely 'pull themselves together' and get better. Without treatment, symptoms can last for weeks, months, or years. Appropriate treatment, however, can help most people with depression. The signs and symptoms of depression include loss of interest in activities that were once interesting or enjoyable, including sex; loss of appetite, with weight loss, or overeating, with weight gain; loss of emotional expression (flat affect); a persistently sad, anxious, or empty mood; feelings of hopelessness, pessimism, guilt, worthlessness, or helplessness; social withdrawal; unusual fatigue, low energy level, a feeling of being slowed down; sleep disturbance and insomnia, early-morning awakening or oversleeping; trouble concentrating, remembering, or making decisions; unusual restlessness or irritability; persistent physical problems such as headaches, digestive disorders, or chronic pain that do not respond to treatment, and thoughts of death or suicide or suicide attempts. The principal types of depression are called major

depression, dysthymia, and bipolar disease (manic-depressive disease).'

Many say people who haven't suffered it will not understand depression even if they were to read a medical description. I have suffered it and still can't explain it. People's experiences of depression can differ greatly. The above explanation gives a lot of signals for depression, but its effects felt like it went much deeper than this.

Differing experiences of depression can be obvious. Some people want a listening ear when depressive feelings arise. Some become socially withdrawn and can't imagine talking with even their closest of friends or relatives. Some people turn to self-harm to release their feelings. Everyone's experience of depression will vary from this in parts, its why it's one of the hardest diseases to live with. People can see a broken arm or when you have a cold. Depression is completely different.

What was depression for me? It's much easier for me to say how I felt.

Depression is...

- Lying in bed, curtains closed, unable to get up.
- Work is impossible – over a 6-month period, I managed one day at work. It didn't work out.
- Speaking to anyone is hard. I feel like a hedgehog wanting to curl up into a ball.
- Happiness is gone – life has nothing positive to offer

- I don't look after myself – any activity is an unachievable goal.
- Insomnia (trouble sleeping), sometimes.
- Hypersomnia (excessive sleeping), sometimes.
- Start skipping events with family and friends.
- Ashamed and embarrassed of feeling this way.
- Constant feeling of nausea – I don't want to eat. I want to eat. I want to drink alcohol.
- Snapping at people, putting my feelings onto them.

Google's Autocomplete 2

Is depression… genetic?
Is depression… a disability?
Is depression… hereditary?
Is depression… a disease?
Is depression… a mental illness?
Is depression… curable?
Is depression… an illness?

Is mental health… a disability?
Is mental health… genetic?
Is mental health… a disease?
Is mental health… hereditary?
Is mental health… a hidden disability?
Is mental health… getting worse?
Is mental health… a disability UK?

Depression is… real
Depression is… killing me

Depression is… a silent killer
Depression is… an illness
Depression is… not a choice
Depression is… ruining my life
Depression is… rage turned inward

Mental health is… important
Mental health is… not fashion
Mental health is… a spectrum of
Mental health is… getting worse
Mental health is… not a weakness
Mental health is… an illness
Mental health is… an excuse

I have highlighted a few that stood out to me that I think need further study.

Is depression… a disability? – It's an interesting question. I never thought about it until I left my job due to long-term sickness. I found that the UK government website stated:

'A mental health condition is considered a disability if it has a long-term effect on your normal day-to-day activity. This is defined under the Equality Act 2010. Your condition is 'long term' if it lasts, or is likely to last, 12 months. 'Normal day-to-day activity' is defined as something you do regularly in a normal day, working set times or interacting with people.

'If your mental health condition means you are disabled you can get support at work from your employer. There are

many different types of mental health condition which can lead to a disability, including dementia, depression, bipolar disorder, obsessive compulsive disorder and schizophrenia.

I wasn't aware of this until researching it. I think it's important people don't suffer in silence and should speak to their employer if they're having issues. There is no point in being unhappy and keeping on going through the motions at work. You have a right to be happy and shouldn't just go through life expecting to conform to what you think the normality of everyday life is. I was guilty of this. I thought there was only the 9–5 and only the time outside work was my own. In reality, I would have to shape work around MY needs.

Is depression… hereditary? – At first, I thought this seemed like a pretty silly question. As I investigated it, I was surprised to find that I wasn't right to think that. There are lots of different studies into this and overall, depression is thought to involve both genetic and environmental factors.

Is depression… a disease? – I found this an interesting question as I had no idea what the answer was. Someone suffering with depression has a clear problem. But if it was a disease, why is it so hard to treat in a medical sense. Just what is it!? Disorder and illness are interchangeably used to describe depression. The Oxford English Dictionary describes each term as the following:

- Disorder – An illness that disrupts normal physical or mental functions.
- Illness – A disease or period of sickness affecting the body or mind.
- Disease – A disorder of structure or function in a human, animal, or plant, especially one that produces specific symptoms or that affects a specific location and is not simply a direct result of physical injury.

Depression would seem to fit under the disease category although it doesn't run along the same lines as, say heart disease or other medical conditions. Depression doesn't simply have a medical solution such as a tablet – anti-depressants are only part of the solution. I don't know, maybe one day there will, but it seems way too complex for that.

It's an interesting debate and one which is debated widely in the medical and psychiatric world.

Is depression… curable? – This links to the question above and I'm sure you can guess the answer. Sadly, depression cannot be 'cured'. This is partly why managing depression and its symptoms, realising the signs and making adjustments in life to deal with it, are so important.

Depression is… killing me – A situation I am familiar with and something I spent a long time saying to myself. At my worst, I saw no hope, and this will be felt by thousands of people every day. A feeling of having so much weighing down on you, exhausting your will to fight and seeing a future where you simply won't be able to carry on.

Depression is… a silent killer – talking about depression is important but a difficult thing to do. I never thought I would be so open to tell my friends about my problems, never mind lay it all out in a book! When it is hidden by a person is when depression is at its most dangerous – when it becomes a 'silent killer'. How many times do we hear of shock suicides in the news today? It's a shock most of the time because we are particularly good at hiding our true feelings. It's something that people need to be aware of.

Depression is… not a choice – it's difficult to grasp sometimes with depression. That sense that, oh get up out of bed and you'll feel fine after an hour or two. Sometimes this just isn't possible, it isn't a choice, because to that person, these options are beyond their control. Coping with depression is more about controlling what you can manage and working from there.

Mental health is… important – There isn't much else to say about this one. MENTAL HEALTH IS IMPORTANT.

Mental health is… getting worse – This could be a single person worrying about their health getting worse or the current issues nationwide regarding mental health. I think people are certainly becoming more aware of these issues and maybe that is due to the issues becoming more prevalent.

Mental health is… an excuse – This was a fear I was having while I wasn't at work. What will people be thinking, is he making excuses to have time off work?

Mood Test

The NHS have a test that anyone can access online to ascertain on a basic level whether they are suffering with depression and anxiety problems. I answered a similar one to this when I attended the GP. I seem to recall the first time I took the test at the doctors was not at the height of my problems. I have filled out the test below as I felt when I was at my worst.

This was a score-based test, applying one of the following numbers to each of the questions below.

1. No, not at all
2. On some days
3. On more than half the days
4. Nearly every day

1. How often have you been bothered by feeling down, depressed or hopeless? 4
2. How often have you had little interest or pleasure in doing things? 4
3. How often have you been bothered by trouble falling or staying asleep, or sleeping too much? 4
4. How often have you been bothered by feeling tired or having little energy? 4
5. How often have you been bothered by poor appetite or overeating? 2
6. How often have you been bothered by feeling bad about yourself, or that you are a failure, or let yourself or your family down? 3

7. How often have you been bothered by trouble concentrating on things, such as reading the newspaper or watching television? 4
8. How often have you been bothered by moving or speaking so slowly that other people could have noticed, or the opposite – being so fidgety or restless that you have been moving around a lot more than usual? 2
9. Have you had an anxiety attack (suddenly feeling fear or panic)? YES
10. How often have you been bothered by feeling nervous, anxious or on edge? 4
11. How often have you been bothered by not being able to stop or control worrying? 3
12. How often have you been bothered by worrying too much about different things? 4
13. How often have you been bothered by having trouble relaxing? 3
14. How often have you been bothered by being so restless that it is hard to sit still? 3
15. How often have you been bothered by becoming easily annoyed or irritable? 4
16. How often have you been bothered by feeling afraid as if something awful might happen? 3
17. Have you been bothered by worrying about any of the following? YOUR HEALTH, YOUR WEIGHT OR HOW YOU LOOK, little or no sexual desire of pleasure during sex, DIFFICULTIES WITH YOUR PARTNER, the stress of taking care of family members, STRESS AT WORK, SCHOOL OR OUTSIDE HOME, BY FINANCIAL PROBLEMS

OR WORRIES, having no one to turn to, SOMETHING BAD THAT HAPPENED RECENTLY, none of the above. *

18. If this questionnaire has highlighted any problems, how difficult have these problems made it for you to do your work, take care of things at home, or get along with other people? Not difficult at all, somewhat difficult, very difficult, EXTREMELY DIFFICULT. *

*Answers in capitals

Depression score – 19/24 – 'Based on your responses to questions 1–8, you are experiencing many symptoms seen in depression.'

Anxiety score – 17/21 – 'Based on your responses to questions 10–16, you are experiencing many symptoms seen in anxiety. This is probably having a big impact on your daily life and you may also be experiencing physical symptoms.'

I decided to retake the test recently and scored much lower. There are still issues that haven't cleared up, but I feel more in control of them now and, much more importantly, I'm fully aware of my issues. Being aware of when you're having a particularly shitty day due to depression, or when you feel a panic attack coming on, is something I found helpful. They happen and they will pass. You are OK.

Anxiety

Gambling was my way of managing anxiety in everyday life. When gambling, I was in a bubble that the anxiety couldn't penetrate. Not a lot could. When everyday life got difficult, I would gamble. This is what addiction is. Needing that fix because that fix is your life. I didn't want it to be my life, but it was.

The 2001–2002 *National Epidemiologic Survey on Alcohol and Related Conditions* suggests that among people with the most severe type of gambling problems – what would be labelled pathological gambling (compulsive/problem gambling) by health professionals – more than 11% are dealing with generalised anxiety disorder, almost 15% are suffering from post-traumatic stress disorder, nearly 22% are dealing with a panic disorder, and 52% are struggling with a specific phobia. I dare say in 2020, the results may be even more alarming as problem gambling has increased.

There are quite a lot of studies done on gambling and mental health which have interesting results. I would suggest searching for these online, they are free to read and offer some science to back up the symptoms for gambling and anxiety/depression.

The problem is when the gambling was taken away from me. The anxiety hadn't gone anywhere, it was a crack that had been papered over.

Just before my first breakdown when I realised I needed help, there were a lot of signs that I didn't see at the time. I clearly remember a day in 2019 when I was going to a festival in Leeds. Just before going, I sat down with my girlfriend and told her I didn't think I could do it. It was slowly creeping up on me, that I was struggling to cope with being in public around lots of people. I hadn't gambled for months; things were good on that front. After talking for a few minutes, we agreed we would go, and I managed the day OK. I was nervous and anxious constantly. I was drinking lots of alcohol. The alcohol was barely servicing the need of stopping the anxiety and all I could think about was going home. The next day I woke up and didn't give it another thought.

The next time I really felt intense anxiety again was a few months later when I was going on holiday to Fuerteventura. On a trip abroad, there are so many times you are surrounded by other people in public. I've got nothing against people, but I was anxious all the time when around them. Airport, flight, restaurants, beaches, bars. People everywhere. When you feel like you just want to be alone, this is a struggle. Again, alcohol was a crutch for me throughout this holiday, alleviating my anxiety when I needed it. But this couldn't go on long term.

I was also having the odd day off work leading up to this while not really having a reason for it. I would just wake up in the night with intense fear and I wouldn't be able to sleep. I would call in work with an excuse and spend the day in bed in fear of the outside world.

Anxiety issues were slightly easier to deal with for me. The medication I was later prescribed by the doctor appeared to have a positive effect and I could apply a lot of what I learned through cognitive behavioural therapy to this issue. Changing thought patterns is important to overcoming anxiety. It's difficult to always expect the worst to happen from any situation. I'm going on a journey, what if I break down on the way? I'm going out in public, what if something bad happens to me? But changing these thoughts with more realistic expectations helped me a lot.

More Strained Relationships?

My relationships with people, family and friends and girlfriends, have always suffered due to my gambling. This was also the case with my depression and anxiety, but I think for different reasons. The gambling was a secret that not many people knew about. I think I was good at hiding it. This meant the few people who did know took the brunt of the negativity from it. I have eventually become much more open about my mental health but still not my gambling.

I have had lots of support with regards to my mental health from so many people that it's made it so much easier on me. And support is what is important. I never wanted help from these people, that was why I was using a doctor and soon after, a counsellor. I just needed people to be there for me for simple things. One friend simply became my gym partner. Another I began to walk with on an evening. I was doing lots of exercise which helped me mentally.

I had to re-evaluate my relationships with everyone.

It's hard because it seems I must distance myself from the hurt I caused people, but not forget everything people have done for me. Remembering the hurt will lead to anger and hate for myself which doesn't help. People can hate me but I'm sure they don't. But I must also allow myself to sit back and say wow, I have some seriously good people in my life who deserve better. They don't deserve me at my worst, they deserve me as the person I truly am. Not the selfish addicted gambler.

The anger and shame I felt got easily passed onto others. Lashing out at people for little or no reason. This needs to be kept under control and I can deal with it a lot better now.

I also think about how it's always easy to feel alone during times of depression. Sitting alone while friends and family and seemingly everyone else is going about their everyday business. But what are people going through that nobody sees. I thought about myself and how many people knew everything that I was going through – not that many as it happens. Don't compare yourself to other people.

Pills

When I first went to the doctor's, they recommended anti-depressants along with links to several websites to address the anxiety I was feeling. I'd never given anti-depressants a second thought before and now I was sat with the doctor with a decision to make. It didn't feel like a difficult decision at the time – if the doctor is recommending it, I thought, *Yes, why not give them a try*? I'll try anything to *fix* how I'm feeling right now. It wasn't until after they were prescribed, and I was researching anti-depressants, that questions started to arise.

Aren't they dangerous? Can't they make suicidal thoughts worse? Don't they block all emotion, not just negative emotion? Doesn't it go against you at work if it's on your medical record? Can't they be addictive? Don't they have lots of dangerous side effects?

Truth is, I didn't know the answer to any of these questions. I accepted my doctor's advice at the time. I didn't realise it was such a big decision. I also think the fact that they weren't guaranteed to work is something I would've liked to have known. Most drugs you take are guaranteed to work against what you're taking them for. Paracetamol for pain or Ibuprofen for inflammation.

Common side effects of my anti-depressants according to the drug company are:

Diarrhoea. Dizziness. Drowsiness. Dyspepsia. Fatigue. Insomnia. Loose stools. Nausea. Tremor. Headache. Paraesthesia. Anorexia. Decreased libido. Delayed ejaculation. Diaphoresis. Ejaculation failure. Xerostomia. Abdominal pain. Agitation. Pain. Vomiting. Anxiety. Hypouricemia. Malaise.

Quite a long list. I'm not quite sure what some of them are! Anxiety also amongst them on the list – something I was taking them for!

I suffered from several of these side effects at first which took months to subside. They were side effects which weren't dangerous but could blight everyday situations.

I eventually got these under control through careful management of my drugs. I think I got lucky overall with this. I've heard of it taking years for people to manage their medication to get the desired results. This backs up the point that mental health and the brain are still an unknown entity in a lot of aspects and varies from person to person quite a bit.

I say I think I got lucky with the drugs working for me, but I also took the therapy side of my recovery seriously and knew how important this was to me moving forward. I didn't particularly want to rely on drugs either as I've always had a slight reluctance to take anything. Even now I'm working towards being able to completely come off the anti-depressants and my dose is relatively low as it stands. On the other hand, I don't want to 'rock the boat' as my anxiety and depression appear to be under control.

I know that for some, they may feel a stigma attached to these drugs. They're taking antidepressants, they must be mental. I've heard people calling them 'mental pills' or 'happy pills'. Anyone I've spoken to seems to know *someone else* who has or is currently taking something similar, and they are happy with their experiences with anti-depressants. I can now be a *someone else*! The drug I take works to affect chemicals in the brain which may be unbalanced in people with depression, panic, anxiety or obsessive-compulsive symptoms. These are the most common anti-depressants which are first administered as they have the fewest complications.

Dreams

'Dreams are often most profound when they seem the most crazy.'

– SF

Dreams fascinate me. I have tended to remember them and, no matter what science says, I do believe eating cheese before bed enhances dream regularity and clarity. A nice chunk of cheddar or cold pizza before bed is always welcome when I'm feeling those late-night hunger pangs.

Since starting to take my medication, I have some of the wildest dreams I've ever experienced. Whether this has any link to the anti-depressants, I don't know. It could be just that I'm sleeping deeper due to my better sleep schedule.

Previously, my dreams were short and uncoordinated. Events would be fast paced and ever-changing. Now they feel like complete parts of real life. My dreams are dragging people up from my past that I hadn't given a second thought for 20 years! They also give me great ideas for if I wanted to start writing a sci-fi novel. I seem to have fewer nightmares than I used to, which is a shame, I didn't mind those!

'The interpretation of dreams is the royal road to a knowledge of the unconscious activities of the mind.'

– SF

Time

Giving myself time to heal was important. As with a physical injury or a virus when the body needs to be rested, the brain needs to be given time to heal. It's hard to accept at first, it goes against a natural way of thinking for me. Surely, I should be forcing myself to get to work, to go outside, face up to my issues. My issues will heal by simply getting used to them.

After a failed attempt at returning to work and more lapses with gambling, I realised I needed to give myself time. Time to do the things that make me happy. Time to manage those days when I didn't feel at my best. Give my time to the therapy and give time for my anti-depressants to start working.

It's easy to feel guilty for not being in work. When I had a meeting about going back to work, I could feel pressure. I know that people who haven't suffered with depression struggle to understand what people who do are going through. And it's not their fault, is it; they are lucky not to have suffered with it. But I knew I had to stay strong and remember what has been making me happy. Don't sacrifice the time I spent.

The time now will prepare me for the future.

You Alright, Mate?

One of the hardest things about dealing with depression and mental health is the fact that there isn't a straightforward guide to dealing with it. You can get recommendations from the doctor and get some pills but how do I deal with everyday life? I'm not at work, should I be expected to be going into work? What do I do at home, I have this spare time but I'm struggling to even get out of bed? I could get therapy but what if I get too anxious to even go?

I spent a lot of time off work due to my depression and anxiety. At first, I will admit, I wasn't doing myself any favours. I spent a lot of time at the pub drinking, thinking it was helping me, not realising I had to help myself. The pub was the only place I was going at first – it was the only place where I was able to use alcohol to relieve my anxieties – sadly, I couldn't take a bottle of rum to the gym!

The pub was, ironically, the stage for probably one of my greatest triumphs. It was the first time I spoke to one of my mates about my problems. I have to say it was very liberating. Wow, people don't judge, people want to help and are understanding and caring. Now, most of my friends know about my struggle with mental illness and are still incredibly supportive of me. We don't often talk about it, the odd 'you alright, mate?' As previously said, support is all that was needed and that's something they offered.

After this, my trips outside the sanctuary of my house could be healthier for my mind and body as I had the support that I needed from friends as well as family. With one of my friends, I would go to the gym and take regular walks. From this, I could build on my life outside of my bedroom and it eventually led me to be able to seek the help I was shying away from.

The Magic Button

'Out of your vulnerabilities will come your strength.'

– SF

Suicide is the leading cause of death among men under the age of thirty-five. A harrowing statistic.

Not the nicest chapter to write, but important all the same to give a picture of my mental state at times. I have already spoken about figures relating to suicide rates and gambling addiction and it's a serious reflection of the problems that arise. I wouldn't say I was close to suicide myself, but I did suffer from suicidal thoughts on a regular basis. I also believe that, had my issues with gambling continued to escalate, suicide would have been on my mind even more.

Have you ever wished there were a magic button which, when pressed, would end your life instantaneously without pain or suffering? This is a feeling I was having, and sometimes still have, at least once a week, when at my lowest. Sitting inside, mostly at night, and feeling hopelessness descend. I would begin to have thoughts of not wanting to be on this earth. A common image in my head is me heading downstairs, walking over to the knife block, selecting the biggest knife and plunging it into my stomach. I sometimes change it up and imagine slitting my wrists in the bath or driving to the nearest bridge and throwing myself off. Or are pills a faster, more painless way to go? The thoughts are fleeting but are a rough mental rollercoaster.

I remember having a conversation about suicide with my friends once. I put on a front when I was with them. This front even made me believe everything was fine. We'd had a few beers and were talking about the usual crap that accompanies ample alcohol intake. I happened to say that 'If it ever looks like I have committed suicide, you need to investigate because I would never think about doing that.' I portrayed a character so well, even I believed what I was saying. I do believe that this is because of the feeling I had a split personality. The gambler and me.

Suicidal thoughts are spared for when I'm at my lowest. When every depressive and anxious thought descends on me at once. It's something I have rarely spoken to anyone about. In fact, I can't really remember speaking to anyone about these thoughts. Being able to deal with this and coming out on the other side, reducing these thoughts and facing them head on when they do occur, is maybe one of my greatest triumphs. I think this because they truly are the darkest times and, in a way, I have been too strong for them.

Split Personality

As mentioned in the previous chapter, I felt like I had a split personality at times when gambling. This personality could be split down further.

The ADDICT

A straightforward if dangerous character. Just waiting for the next opening to gamble. A selfish thinker.

The SECRET GAMBLER

The man will do anything to keep anyone from finding out about the addiction. If anything, there is no addiction.

The LIAR

Sadly, works very well in unison with The Addict. Will tell any lies to keep The Addict fed.

The MISER

The stranger who turns up when all money is lost. Suddenly money is worth something!?

The INTELLIGENT

This person knows what's being done is wrong but is shouted down by the rest.

The ANGRY

Easily angered by others, as his name suggests. Wants to do what he wants; however wrong he may be.

The VULNERABLE

The character who comes out when feeling hopeless.

Therapy

When did I decide therapy was needed and that I wasn't going to find answers at the bottom of a pint glass in the pub?

I had completed my cognitive behavioural therapy but was suddenly faced with something different. That first day waking up after a summer holiday and not being able to set off to work is still clear in my mind. It hit me like a tonne of bricks. It had obviously been slowly building in the background and the pressure was at breaking point. It's something I had learned from CBT. Letting my feelings about gambling build had many times led to a massive splurge of betting eventually.

The day before going back to work, I had spent the day watching England win the Cricket World Cup, enjoying myself, oblivious of what was to come. I woke up the next day and got ready for work as normal, fully dressed, tie et al, ready to step out of the door. Before I knew what was happening, I was sat downstairs, my head in hands, crying my eyes out. I'm not much of a crier. This was serious.

I was at the doctors later that day being given a 2-week sick note for anxiety and depression and getting prescribed anti-depressants.

After a couple of months off work with no improvements in my condition and ever-increasing dosages of anti-depressants, it was time for me to seek help. I searched around and found a therapist in the same village as mine who advertised the help I thought I needed. I took a chance and I booked in for a free consultation. I met up with her for an hour and she talked about what services she offered. It seemed to be what I was wanting. She offered hour sessions for £40 and would use an array of techniques based on my needs and what would work, and with a dash of humour which I appreciated. This was going to be a lot different to my CBT sessions and I had no idea how this was going to work.

The anti-depressants I was prescribed were helping with my anxiety but not really dealing with my depressive state. I felt I was spiralling out of control and the hole I was in seemed too deep to climb out of. I wanted the therapy to get to the bottom of this. I wanted to be happier. Everything had become a struggle; I wasn't enjoying anything in life.

After my initial couple of sessions of counselling, I was exhausted and worried it wasn't going to work for me. I now see that my main issue was the fact I wasn't aware of how counselling worked. This wasn't necessarily my fault. I was expecting to sit and tell my counsellor a load of facts about my addiction and anxieties, and she would have an answer. This wasn't the case. It was going to be the first time in my life where I was going to sit down, put everything out on the table, and talk about my feelings.

Never in my life had I ever really thought about my feelings. I'm good at stating facts about myself but I found it difficult to express and describe my feelings. For several sessions, I probably seemed like a closed book. My counsellor explained she could see I had issues as I would give signals when talking, but it was a case of discovering what these were. She could see the happiness I felt in myself, which was probably partly a mask and partly my natural character. But after years of hiding my feelings and lying about my gambling, it was time to lift the barrier up.

Having therapy would also instantly answer my biggest question at the time – when I should go back to work. My therapist told me not to worry about this and she assured me I'd know when the time was right. This was a weight off my shoulders. I could now concentrate on getting better.

NHS

I had initially contacted the NHS at first, through my doctor, to try and secure an appointment with a member of their mental health team. I was questioned quite substantially over the phone as part of the process, but I was turned down for an appointment. This was difficult to take but I realised that the NHS was taking on what they thought were the most important cases – I have read a news article about how mental health was underfunded. I took the news on the chin and decided to get help privately. This was a tough decision due to the cost of therapy and my considerable debt but luckily, I was able to get help from my parents. I know there are some people who might not get this help.

Me, Myself and I

Seeing a therapist was the first time I really started to understand the concept of looking after myself and my mental health. Sometimes, I would let the pressure of life take priority over my own mental health. It's easy to do, especially for someone who didn't really understand what this meant.

I used to see no difference between selfishness and looking after one's self. It can be the smallest of things that contribute to this, but I found it important to understand what makes me happy now. Give yourself the time for what you want, stop putting everything else before personal happiness. I'm not talking about being selfish but working in a job I wasn't enjoying was an example of this. The place I was spending five days a week was draining my happiness. I'd get home from work and struggle to get out walking or to the gym. I needed to free up time to do the things that make me happy.

What Are You Feeling?

As mentioned, the hardest thing for me during therapy was telling the therapist how I felt. It was clear from the first few sessions that I would struggle with this. It may just have been my misjudgement over what a therapist does, or it may have been due to a struggle within myself. I wasn't used to expressing how I felt at all. I would sit down for an hour telling her facts about my life but would rarely be able to explain how these situations made me feel. This wasn't a surprise to her; she said a lot of people struggle with this and that she would try different approaches to get me to ‘reveal myself’. The one which happened to work best seemed gimmicky at first but was able to unlock things that I didn’t realise were in my head. I knew they were there, it’s why I was having therapy, but I never focused on them at all. It felt amazing to finally understand what was going on.

It was a few sessions in when my therapist decided to try out some cards with expressive feelings on, which were used to enable me to express my feelings.

These were a pack of cards, similar in size to playing cards, but instead of the usual faces, each card had a picture on them displaying an emotion or feeling. Everything ranging from sunshine and curvy lines to red exclamation marks and large onomatopoeic words.

I was handed the cards and told to shuffle through – I assure you this isn’t a magic trick – and identify any which resembled how I felt. After a short silence in the room while I sifted through them, I came across three which I thought reflected how I felt perfectly. I have always been more of a visual person and this may have been why it worked better than simply trying to talk about my feelings. Discovering my feelings and interpreting them was going to be hard but necessary.

The three cards I chose from the pack were:

Number 1, the word ‘ARRRRRRGGGGGHHHH HHH’. I think this depicted what I felt if I thought about my situation. I would literally feel like screaming, angry at myself for everything I had done.

Number 2, a series of jagged red lines. Again, if I were to draw my feelings, this fitted perfectly. Anger, screaming, red. If I closed my eyes, a lot of the time this is what I would see.

Number 3, a red jagged outline drawing of a person. This again, reflected the anger I felt in me.

My therapist asked what I want the cards to look like? I told her I wanted the lines to be soft, wavy and blue. I wanted to feel calm again. But for now, I had to deal with what I was feeling…

ANGER.

Anger… and Shame

A famous piece of analysis from Freud, and one which I could apply to my own feelings, was that depression was anger turned inward.

The 'feeling cards' revealed that I was angry. It was now time to address these feelings. What was there that I was angry at?

I was angry at the situation I had gotten myself into through gambling. Every time I was getting somcwhere in life, I would make it harder and harder for myself. Money in the bank? You can wave that goodbye in the space of a few minutes. Every time this happened, a hatred grew for myself. I don't hate anyone else in the world, but I did hate him. Myself, but almost another part of myself. It wasn't me; it was a character that I shared my life with. He couldn't control himself. I had to keep reminding myself, I am more powerful than him.

I was angry at the fact I had spent 12 years throwing money away. Angry at myself, full of resentment for what I had made of my life. I will never be able to live those 12 years again and get all the money back I had lost. I hate myself.

Recognising this anger and getting it out on the table, was the first step in overcoming it. I couldn't continue to ignore it just because it made me uncomfortable.

The intense hatred for myself on one side was offset by a feeling of shame. The anger was an intense emotion. The shame felt like a cool, cold emotion which crippled me in a corner. I felt more vulnerable than I'd ever felt before in my whole life. It was this which stopped me wanting to interact with family and friends. I felt paranoid ALL of the time. What if someone finds out what I've done, how could I live with that? What if people have worked out that I'm a gambling addict? Everyone else is getting on with their lives and I'm stuck in a hole. I dragged around the feeling of shame. How had I done this to myself and my family. I had put them through so much and they didn't deserve any of it.

It was what I would choose to do with these feelings that would decide how I moved on and improve my mental health. The fact I had got these out in the open, I could now put work in to stop these feelings eating away at me. The fact I was reminded at every turn about what I had done was weighing me down. I was faced with the sizeable debt and the fact I was still living at home and these were reminders of what I had done. In discovering these feelings, it was important to change the way I felt about myself and gambling.

A Change of Perspective

There were various ways in which counselling began to turn my life around. It wasn't all plain sailing; the sessions were intense and after my early sessions, I was emotionally exhausted, and it took a lot of energy from me. It helped that I wasn't in work. I could de-stress by doing the things that helped me – gym, walking, writing, drawing.

Once we had identified my feelings, I began to look at myself, gambling and my mental health differently. I had so much running around relentlessly in my head, most of the time without realising it, sometimes just recognising it was increasing my anxieties.

The main thing my counsellor helped me accept was that the work I had done for 6 months in reducing my gambling was a big step I should be proud of. I had for so long felt I had nothing to be proud of. I was hard on myself constantly, carrying with me the anger, shame and embarrassment. Proof was in the fact that in the early sessions I struggled to accept these positives, constantly feeling like I 'deserved to be punished.' I almost felt embarrassed to be told I should be proud of myself. Again, why was I thinking like this? It was time for me to accept what happened, not live the rest of my life with regret. Change my perspective of things completely.

'When I am criticized, I can defend myself, but I'm powerless against the praise.'

– SF

One problem which would crop up from the beginning of my sessions was the debt I had to gambling. It is a worry which fed my addiction for a long time. However, once my counsellor helped me realise that my debt was decreasing and not gambling was helping to reduce the debt, it was something I was able to accept. Again, that change of perspective was massive for me.

I always focused on relationships which had broken down due to my gambling, both romantic relationships and friendships. Not everyone can cope with the stresses that gambling brings, and I just couldn't understand how to cope with people who walked away. I couldn't see things from their point of view. It wasn't until I started to see this differently that I could stop regretting relationships that broke down. It is hard and I am sorry to people I have hurt but I can understand their decisions as well now.

When I had my initial time off work, I felt almost guilty. I didn't understand mental health at all and felt like I should be expecting myself to get back to work after a couple of months. My counsellor was the first person to make it clear that I would know when my time to return to work would be. I had tried to return early before I sought counselling, and this only led to more problems having had only one day at work. To realise that my mental health came before a lot of things was important.

During my time off work, it was the first time I'd broached the subject of mental health with my friends. Initially, I had hidden it from them. This was because I didn't know how to talk to them, in fear of how they'd take it and also because I was seeing them less and less due to my depression. It took a couple of pints of beer in me, but I eventually told a close friend. His reaction was comforting. I had eventually told all my close friends and the support I had, as mentioned earlier, was incredible. I remind myself, during the Middle Ages, mentally ill people were seen to be under the influence of the devil or other evil spirits – it would have been a damn site harder telling someone about your problems back then!

Something else I need to keep reminding myself is I'm 31 years old. Still young enough to turn my life around completely, take different paths, make more mistakes and learn from them. It's something I have always been cautious of – failure. I haven't wanted to try new things because I was scared of what will happen if it doesn't go to plan. I've come to realise I can't live my life thinking like that.

A change of perspective on my actions was a big change and something I have to remind myself of to this day. This almost comes automatically to me now.

19 Years Old

As much as The Courteeners argue the opposite, I found myself in a weird age freeze for many years. What do I mean by this? As I discussed with my therapist, at 30 years old, I was still feeling like I was 19 years old, the age when I first started gambling. As I gambled, I found that I couldn't move on with my life. A lack of money was one reason for this and the effect on my relationships was another. I couldn't hold together meaningful relationships which had a future. I couldn't move out from my parents' home; I just didn't have the funds.

My therapist helped me understand this situation and at least made me feel like it wasn't a strange occurrence for someone with my background. She also confirmed that I could fix it by moving forward now.

How Happy Are You?

I was asked this question at the start of most of my therapy sessions. I would be asked to rate my happiness level from one to ten, ten being happiest. At first, this seemed to be the most open-ended question ever. Plucking a number out of thin air to rate my happiness. The first few times I was asked, I'd look down at my feet or stare blankly at the wall. Eventually, I'd come out with an answer 'err, five?'. I'd pose my answer as a question, have I done this properly. Oh, I've got the answer wrong but – I feel like shit – 50 percent seemed a good answer. Well, it turns out there wasn't a wrong answer, and this was a good way to measure happiness when it's compared week on week. It was important to look at the highs and lows and what in life was affecting my happiness.

During my worst I could be as low as a two, during my best maybe up to an eight. But in truth I would be happy living my life at a solid middle ground. In asking this question, my therapist wasn't expecting me to ever say, I'm a ten, my life is fixed. We will all have days when we're feeling rubbish. Life is a rollercoaster after all. I would be happy just not having massive swings in happiness. Being unbelievably happy one day and contemplating suicide the next isn't a good way to live. This is the hardest thing to deal with. It mirrors the feeling when I gambled – the incredible highs and the gut-wrenching lows.

Asking myself this question now my therapy has ended is just as effective. If I wake up and feel like a four, I can ask myself why I think I feel like this. What can I do right now to increase this number? What can I do to make sure I don't wake up tomorrow feeling the same? The same if I wake up an eight. You're feeling good, what can I do to increase my chances of waking up tomorrow feeling like an eight?

Simple but effective.

Panic Attacks

I had never suffered a panic attack until I was 31 years old. At the time I had no idea what was happening. A mixture of taking too much caffeine and performing an intense leg workout at the gym had led to it. I was laid down in a leg press machine and was climbing out when I felt my heart racing and a sudden dream-like detachment from the gym and my workout partner. What exactly did I feel?

1. Wow, my heart is racing faster than usual.
2. OK, that can't be right, can it? I can hear it pounding in my head.
3. What is this feeling creeping over me?
4. My face is numb, my mouth tingling. I feel dizzy and nauseas.
5. OK, am I going faint or maybe dying? An intense fear begins to grow within me.

6. OK, I need help, my heart is about to burst. I begin to think of an ambulance coming to collect me.
7. I head to an empty, dark room. I lie down. Breathe, in and out. I tremble as I lay there.
8. I close my eyes, concentrating on my breathing.
9. You're OK. My training partner comes in and gives me some reassuring words.
10. And, it has passed. A sense of relief creeps over me.

I think a lot of people know that feeling of euphoria when you think you've escaped something serious. I guess, in fact, my life wasn't in danger, but it felt like it was at the time. I can compare the feeling to a time when I had been surfing (badly) in Newquay and I got swept out to sea by a rip tide. I was fine in the end. That night though, I walked around Newquay with my eyes wide open like I was baby witnessing the world through brand new eyes and everything was new and interesting. The sheer panic I felt and great relief when I made it back to shore were such intense emotions.

My second panic attack came within a few days of the first one. It was still as frightening as the first. Of course, panic attacks like the ones I went through aren't life threatening although I knew I needed to ensure I wasn't doing anything to encourage them to the point they were affecting my life.

It was time to cut back on caffeine before the gym. Since doing this I have not experienced another attack. I also address my anxiety as much as possible to make sure it doesn't lead to something similar in the future.

The Brain Bunker

You're safe inside your own head. Protected from outside influence. Protected from the opinions of others. And, your brain knows best. Right? I noticed this wasn't always a good thing for me and a lot of the time, cutting off outside influences had a profound negative effect.

I've found that I've spent a lot of my time listening to the voice that narrates life inside my head. This was certainly the case while gambling. The voice that says, 'fuck it, have one more bet'. Not always negative like this, but it can, a lot of the time, become toxic for your mental state. I started to believe things were possible, started to believe things that are bullshit. 'Have one bet and then you can walk away' – really? When had this ever happened?

Talking to yourself, you can easily start to question everything and every thought in life. This highlights the inherent stresses that come with gambling. What if I can never afford a house? What if people find out about my gambling? All this leads to more gambling – a vicious cycle. And since when were thoughts always fact? They're not.

In reality, we know that what we think isn't always true, but that doesn't stop it. I had so much internal thinking that I was jeopardising my life. The best way to combat, I eventually realised, was to talk outside of your head, something that I didn't do for years, and a hard habit to break. Cognitive behavioural therapy helped me do this but it's still a struggle to this day. When I'm alone and thoughts are whizzing around my head, it's still difficult. Even writing this book is a good way to combat this problem though. Learn to talk to people or write a diary or a book. Get things out of you head. Don't let them build up. Over time they will burst out in a more negative way when the pressure becomes too much.

Apparently, some people don't have the little narrator in their head, which would be weird for me to experience. What voice tells them they can make that jump over a 3-foot wall while pissed?

I Can Deal with Anything

I can deal with anything.

These simple five words were a big help early on in my therapy sessions. They seemed to reinforce that I would come through this bad time of my life. I knew I could because I'd been in a place before all this started when I could deal with anything. I would try to repeat them at any time I was feeling anxious or stressed. This was occurring a lot at the time. Any situation outside of my bedroom was difficult. It's hard to explain the feeling to anyone who hasn't suffered with depression and anxiety.

I had lots of activities I enjoyed doing which weren't realistic goals once my anxiety and depression had kicked in. The simplest of pleasures like getting out for a walk weren't within reach. A feeling of being anxious around other people, fearing encountering people I work with wanting to ask questions. I needed to take small steps.

It was summer, a great time for getting outside. Eventually, I bit the bullet and began taking short walks with my family in the nearby woods. It's what I enjoy. Breathing in the air, feeling close to nature ('talking to the trees' as my therapist put it). Where I live in Yorkshire has views to rival any in the world. The woods were a quiet place with only a few people there. It was the start of my recovery.

Next on the list was the gym. A bit more difficult at times as it was a busier place with lots of interaction with people. The people are nice though, easy to get on with. The gym is also a place where people enjoy the same ideology – there's a reason why they are there – it makes them happy. It wasn't long before I was able to go to the gym without feelings of anxiety.

Any obstacle I overcame reinforced those words…

I can deal with anything.

'Flowers are restful to look at. They have neither emotions nor conflicts.'

– SF

The Small Things

'Look into the depths of your own soul and learn first to know yourself, then you will understand why this illness was bound to come upon you and perhaps you will thenceforth avoid falling ill.'

– SF

There are lots of *small things* which I have learned make me happier. Things which I didn't give enough time to previously or simply didn't appreciate as I do now. These can be little things or bigger things but things I know I need to make time for in my life. The little things are often helpful when I'm not feeling great. These things are similar to the distraction techniques which I utilise for CBT, which is useful, and are in no particular order.

Making a cup of coffee. Taking a bath or shower. Getting outside for a walk and taking on hiking challenges. Going to the gym. Watching films. Seeing my girlfriend. Talking to and spending time with friends. Writing this book. Reading. Sketching anything and everything. Bowling. Eating chicken nuggets. Eating cheese and crackers. Eating pizza. Eating… OK, this could go on for a while, you get the point. Having a cider, beer or wine – within reason! Playing darts. Playing board games. Watching football.

The (Negative) Small Things

As with everything, there is another side, and for the positives, there is also a list of negatives which impact upon my mental health. These include: Binging on alcohol. Caffeine tablets – extremely bad for anxiety! Gambling – an obvious one! Stressful situations. Forgetting to take care of myself. Lack of socialising. Lack of routine. Not communicating, sealing myself off. Lack of a sleeping pattern. Winter, cold, lack of sun and fresh air.

Exercise

Not the answer to depression, but certainly a part of it. After my initial bouts of being bed-bound and when I was eventually ready to go outside again, I began walking more and attending the gym regularly. This has done wonders for my mental health, in conjunction with my tablets, therapy and everything else.

A post workout endorphin hit, and general healthy eating should not be overlooked. It was a big part of what has saved me.

Pandemic

I'm currently stuck inside in isolation while I write this part of my book due to the coronavirus pandemic. It has got me thinking a lot about everyone's mental health during this time. People being isolated in their homes, not looking after their mental health, not having a routine to stick to – and having a lot of spare time to gamble online! I had many months prior to this where I was stuck at home with depression and anxiety and at the point lockdown occurred, ironically, I was fairly comfortable being at home with an effective routine to stick to.

Routine is so important for a lot of people in situations like this. I know this and still struggle sometimes to stick to one. To lose routine is to lose meaning in life. It can lead to boredom, alcohol, panic and a lack of perspective. Writing this book regularly keeps my mind active. Having a workout routine at home while the gyms are closed helps to keep my brain chemistry and interaction with my anti-depressants in check. Also making use of my one piece of permitted public exercise a day is helping! There's nothing like an endorphin hit after a workout or a walk!

As mentioned previously, the situation made me think about gambling. Not in a negative way for myself necessarily, but I was thinking about people with a lot of free time turning to online gambling to pass the time. Casinos and bookies are closed for the foreseeable future, along with restaurants and leisure centres and pubs and any other areas where the general public are likely to gather unnecessarily. One article I read brought the heart-breaking news that some bookies were already posting some losses due to the virus. Of course, I say this in jest, but I know this is not ideal for their employees. However, I'm sure the companies, who consistently post millions of pounds of profit a month will survive, when compared to struggling small businesses.

The closing of casinos and bookies will, of course, drive some customers towards online gambling. There are several bookies who are certainly trying to do this. I have had several emails with a 'helpful reminder' that even though their shops are shut, I can still gamble online. It's the last email a gambling addict wants to receive when they're stuck inside with time on their hands. Pubs are closed so drinking at home may become an issue and facilitates gambling even more. Also, with uncertainty over jobs, people may be more prone to the 'I can make some money on the side here by gambling' mentality.

Online gambling is probably the most dangerous type of gambling as well. There are so many gambling companies to choose from. Stopping a problem gambler from gambling is almost impossible if they really want to gamble. With so much time on their hands, the destruction could be devastating to their lives. And if they are in a hole in terms of gambling, there's no way to get away from it. They are stuck inside and can't do much to improve their mental health in that moment.

While listening to the radio during one gloomy day inside, I happened upon an interesting discussion about sports betting and gambling in general during the coronavirus pandemic. I think the underlying premise of the discussion was how the virus was negatively impacting upon the sports betting industry. How would a seemingly 'recession proof' industry cope with the lack of sports during this time. On the weekend of the 28th / 29th March 2020, there was tiny fraction of the football matches that would usually be going ahead at the 'business end' of the football season. A few games dotted around Europe in Sweden and Belarus but not a whole lot more worldwide. It's the same with other sports, barely anything happening in the sporting world. Surely this is having a major negative impact on the gambling industry.

You would be right to suspect this, until it was pointed out by a guy in the studio, a statistic from Italy. Italy is suffering a lot from the outbreak and strict curfews are keeping people inside most of the time. So, this guy said that in Italy, online poker play had risen by 50% during this time. And this is my point – **GAMBLERS WILL ALWAYS FIND A WAY TO GAMBLE!** And gambling companies are all too happy to prey on people when at their most vulnerable.

It's a hard time. I'm trying to keep busy, working out in my garage instead of the gym and keeping busy writing and sketching. It's easy for the mind to drift to negative thoughts and thoughts of gambling when there is little to keep it stimulated. It doesn't help that I'm currently searching for a job. Not the best economic climate to be doing this. But it also keeps my mind busy, being able to work on my CV and job hunt online.

I never thought something like this would happen. Yes, I was aware pandemics are possible and have happened before, but we take things like health for granted. We take going to the pub on a Saturday night for granted. Simple acts of love like seeing an elderly relative. These all got taken away in an instant, almost overnight. And it takes time to adjust and be proactive in making sure we look after ourselves.

The next step is a constantly moving target at the moment. Almost daily updates from Prime Minister Boris Johnson and the measures the government are taking. Uncertain times are ahead, but it's important to not get anxious and take every day as it comes. The latest news is the inevitable 'lockdown' which is restricting movement outside of homes to only what is necessary. I can see the impacts of this virus to be massive in the following months in all areas of society.

Doing absolutely nothing never felt so difficult…

Lapse

Lapses have happened in my recovery, both in terms of gambling and mental health. Depression is expected to rear its ugly head every now and again. Calling this a lapse is probably not the appropriate word. Accepting depression will return briefly, recognising the signs when it is happening and understanding it won't last forever is all part of dealing with this. Decreasing the size of the mood swings is the best that I hope for and I can accept this.

Lapses in gambling are harder to manage and deal with if they occur. They would affect my mental health and my situation financially.

The bottom line is, I will do everything I can in my power to not gamble. A lapse must not become a relapse. As I am now, I feel confident of neither lapsing nor relapsing. But there were times when I wasn't so sure.

Even during my recovery, I was still struggling with gambling and this was something that helped me see the 'light at the end of the tunnel'. I had been thinking for a week, on and off, about gambling and 'testing myself', and on the Friday night of that week, I finally gave in and placed a bet on the dark seductress that was basketball total points betting. By the end of the following week, I had lost a lot of money. In that time, I had made enough to pay off all my current debt but once again had not been able to stop when ahead. I was physically sick during this period – my gambling had returned and had plunged me once again into darkness. I knew I had to see my therapist and make sense of this – why had I gambled, does this mean CBT and counselling isn't for me, will I be a gambling addict forever? These were just a few of the irrational but genuine thoughts I had at the time. This is when I learned about what is called a lapse. This is not a relapse – a return to gambling like before – a lapse is more like a brief struggle, something which my therapist assured me was something she'd seen before and not unusual. In that session and after it I was very emotional – the weight lifted from my mind was massive. For some reason, it brought everything I had been doing to that point into focus and I realised I was a work in progress, but I was heading in the right direction.

I have no delusions about gambling going forward. I realise that my aims through CBT and counselling were to never gamble again – I never again wanted to be in the position where I was starting out with some small bets thinking I could control it. My brain will always link back to the addiction in the end. Now I look at gambling in a completely different way. When I look at football fixtures, I don't think I can predict the score line due to past results, I look at it and know no one can predict such things.

Another Lapse

Oh, for fuck's sake… It's happened again. I accept it and start at day 1, *again*.

For me, counting days that I had been gamble-free didn't help. This seemed to only add pressure. As the days increased, I wouldn't be able to stop thinking about gambling and this often led to a lapse. If I concentrated too much on gambling, it would often lead me astray, trapping me in a mindset from the past. I hadn't been gamble-free for more than 90 days in the years from 2008 to 2019. I know certain addiction guides promote counting days of sobriety – it's just something that doesn't work for me.

I'm not even going to reveal in this book how long I have been gamble-free. I know the date of the last time I gambled but I don't focus on this.

My Tips

Tip 1 – REMEMBER WHY YOU DON'T GAMBLE AND ALWAYS THINK OF OTHERS. BE HONEST IN EVERYTHING YOU DO AND ACCOUNTABLE IN YOUR ACTIONS

Tip 2 – SPEND MORE TIME WITH YOUR FAMILY AND FRIENDS. DISTRACT YOURSELF THROUGH HEALTHY MEANS AS MUCH AS POSSIBLE

Tip 3 – SPEND LESS TIME ON YOUR LAPTOP AND PHONE AND MORE TIME JOURNALING YOU THOUGHTS AND FEELINGS

Tip 4 – PAY DEBTS AS THEY FALL DUE AND PUT EVERYTHING INTO CLEARING THE GAMBLING DEBTS

Tip 5 – REMEMBER – GAMBLING IS NOT A WAY TO MAKE MONEY – DIRECT EFFORT TO OTHER VENTURES, MAYBE THOSE WHICH CAN HELP OTHERS LIKE YOU. MAYBE EVEN FIX PAST ACTS OF SELFISHNESS AND BECOME MORE SELFLESS

Tip 6 – COMMUNICATION – IF YOU'RE STRUGGLING, TALK TO SOMEONE. A THERAPIST OR OTHER RECOVERING GAMBLERS OR JUST FRIENDS AND FAMILY

Tip 7 – DISTANCE YOURSELF FROM EVERY ASPECT OF GAMBLING AS MUCH AS POSSIBLE

Tip 8 – PRACTICE CBT AS MUCH AS POSSIBLE

Tip 9 – BE GRATEFUL FOR WHAT YOU DO HAVE. DON'T LIVE LIFE BASED ON WHAT YOU THINK IS EXPECTED OF YOU

Tip 10 – STRUGGLING? TAKE AWAY YOUR MEANS OF GAMBLING ASAP. LIMIT ACCESS TO MONEY AS WELL. DON'T GO LOOKING FOR YOUR ROCK BOTTOM. FIX IT NOW!

Gamstop

I have only just registered with GAMSTOP at 31 years old. It's one of the best options available to problem gamblers which, when used in conjunction with other things, is highly effective for preventing gambling. I was doing some research into new gambling regulations being introduced and at the bottom of one article I was reading was an advertisement for registering with GAMSTOP. I was always reluctant to sign up with GAMSTOP as I thought it was a monthly subscription service. It was either that or the fact I subconsciously didn't want to prevent myself from gambling. Anyway, it turns out that this is a free service to sign up with.

GAMSTOP allows controls to be put in place to restrict gambling activities online. It prevents the use of websites and apps run by gambling companies in Great Britain for a period of your choosing – this can be 6 months, a year or even 5 years. During this time, the block cannot be taken off. Signing up takes only a few minutes. In order to sign up, all that is required is a few details to confirm your identification.

GAMSTOP only applies to online gambling, however, other exclusion services can be used for gambling offline such as playingsafe.org.uk for casinos and self-exclusion.co.uk for betting shops and bookmakers. I have personally never really gone into bookies, but the casino exclusion is useful to me.

I think there will be a lot of people who are currently addicted to gambling, who want to stop, but can't find that first step to help them. I think GAMSTOP can provide that. As I said previously, wanting to stop and stopping are completely different. GAMSTOP and other similar services can provide the first step in stopping. Also, my bank has a service which, if opted in, can stop a bank card being used for gambling transactions. This may also be helpful for people looking to stop.

In further good regulatory news, ALL British gambling websites will have to participate in the GAMSTOP self-exclusion scheme and offer it to all customers from 31 March 2020.

Even though I only signed up to it recently, it still felt like another weight had been lifted off my shoulders. As I always say, a dedicated gambling addict will always find a way to gamble. Obstacles like this, however, present a chance for people to stop completely. A chance to delay that decision and to think about the choices. That's all life is. A bunch of choices. Take your time, choose wisely and happiness can bloom in the face of adversity.

Part III – Future Happiness

Happiness

What is happiness? The Oxford English Dictionary tells us it's 'the state of being happy'.

Obviously…

'What is happy?' might be a better question. The Oxford English Dictionary tells us this is 'feeling or showing pleasure or contentment'.

A bit clearer…

What can we pick up from the dictionary definition of happy? From what I can tell:

1. It can be both felt and shown. Feeling happiness. Showing happiness. This seems straightforward. It also came with complications for me. I would show happiness to hide my true feelings.
2. It is a state and not a personality trait. Happiness comes and goes in other words. Nobody is 100% happy all the time. I think it is important that we are aware of this. It might seem obvious but sometimes we strive for things that aren't possible.

How important is it that we are happy? I personally feel like my happiness is so important right now. When I'm unhappy, I start to worry about my gambling past. When I'm happy, my anxieties disappear, I don't feel I have to gamble anymore. As long as I know I can't associate gambling with happiness then I feel safe.

I know it is hard to control my happiness but there's lots I can do to give myself the best chance at being happy.

The Many Faces of Me

Sometimes, it's inevitable I have discussions with myself inside my head, no matter how hard I try to stop. Maybe when I'm lying in bed trying to get to sleep at 2am or maybe when I'm sat in my car driving alone on a long journey. When they do happen, I make sure I'm prepared to stay in control. If distraction is not possible, I rely on what I have learned. What does 'happy me' suggest?

Happy me: I'm really enjoying life. I'm staying fit. I'm looking for a new occupation. I'm proud of how far I have come. I want to do the best I can, make people proud of me. I would love to help other people who are struggling with mental health and addiction. I want to have fun with the people I love.

I've just borrowed my bank card from my mum to make a payment online.

The Gambler: This is my chance. Note down the debit card details. I can join up to a casino later. I can have a gamble later, make a bit of money. It'll make me happy, relieve any stresses.

Happy Me: You're not noting it down. You're giving your bank card back. You know why you're giving it back. When has doing this ever made you happy? When have you ever made money? Think of your past and now your future goals. Give the card back now. Done.

Alcohol Me: I can't gamble, I'm in debt. I'm going to drink a shit load of alcohol, get blind drunk and forget my problems.

Happy Me: You're not going to drink to get pissed. Have a drink with family and friends if you want. But drink is just a small part of your life now. You know how you'll feel tomorrow if you drink too much. You know that binge drinking often leads to gambling and increases anxiety and feelings of depression. It will not make you happy in the long run. Stay in control and be happy with that. You have a happy life.

Depressed Me: I can't get out of bed. I want to curl up. I can't face anyone today. I feel awful.

Happy Me: It's OK. You're OK. Take it easy. One step at a time. Can you get up and take a shower or make a cup of tea? No pressure if you can't. This will happen. It will pass.

Suicidal Me: You're in mountains of debt. You've let everyone down. There's no point to life anymore. I might as well kill myself. I don't want to be here anymore. I want to go for a drive and never come home.

Happy Me: Stop this thinking right away. You've come so far and have such a long journey ahead of you. Lots of chances at moving forward. Think about everything you've learned about yourself. You've got this.

Anxious Me: I don't want to go out. I'm anxious about being around people. What if this happens? What if that happens?

Happy Me: You can deal with anything. Your thoughts don't rule you. Thoughts aren't fact.

Happy Me: I am the strongest out of all of us. Any decision to be made is made by me and this will always be the case from now on. I will not allow you to gamble. I will help you when you're feeling depressed. I will help you when you're feeling anxious. I will keep us happy.

My Experiences

I've had quite a few people, including my therapist, ask whether my experiences with gambling and mental health would make me want to consider helping people in a similar position in the future. My initial thought is that I would jump at the chance to be involved in something. It's a subject I feel so strongly about due to my struggle. It's also a subject I think I have a lot of knowledge on, based on what I've been through.

From being in the thick of things for years, I know that funding and support for problem gambling is far behind what it should be. Stricter regulations are being put in place currently, but these are not keeping pace with the problems. As I'm fully aware from my own experiences, a gambler will always find a way to gamble. More funding should be put into helping these people as well as stricter regulations being put in place. Stopping these issues before they begin is the only way to stop stories such as mine and many others.

We know improvements are happening with regards to regulations, but I just feel it needs to be stepped up a gear. Tighter regulations can stop people getting into the place I was. In terms of support, I chose to keep things to myself so I could carry on gambling. Stricter regulations can stop enabling problem gamblers to feed their addiction.

Tighter regulations are now in place surrounding machines in bookmakers and using credit cards for gambling online. But what else could be done? Enforced betting limits online would be a good place to start. However, I also know that betting companies bring in a lot of taxes for the UK and passing major regulations limiting betting company's profits will be difficult. Look at smoking. It also has zero benefits and is addictive and dangerous for health and yet is still around.

Better checks on source of funds should be in place. You should not be able to use loans to fund gambling. Checks should be done from the beginning as well – not after a gambler has lost thousands of pounds.

Welfare of players appears to be bottom of the list of priorities for bookies. I know this for a fact. The automated social responsibility emails are pathetic and even when a human emailed and asked if I was comfortable with the amount I was gambling, a simple reply of 'yes' was enough to carry on and lose thousands more to them. And as I've said previously, restrictions on deposits are always queried when the money has already been lost.

In terms of helping problem gamblers, I have already said it is underfunded through the NHS. Of course, when looking for help, there are private places like the Priory, but this route is expensive, especially for people in debt, which gamblers can inherently be.

And what about young people? I think one of the most astounding things I have come to realise is how many young people have been seduced by gambling. Is there enough done to stop the cycle ever beginning? More education is needed in this respect. I don't think young people are aware of the implications of gambling. They are also being seduced from a young age. I have seen lots of stories about kids playing video games and being able to electronically pay for loot boxes, cases, chests, bundles and card packs. They are, in essence, virtual games of chance which can be purchased in games. This has most likely been the main contributing factor in the small rise in problem gambling among children. It's a dangerous concept and can cause implications for generations ahead.

I have come to think, how could I use my knowledge to aid problem gamblers? A charity? A funded counselling service? It's something I'm certainly looking into and will consider in the future.

Another step I'd like to make in the future is telling those friends and family who aren't aware about my gambling problems. All of them know about my battle with mental health issues but few know about my gambling experiences. Maybe this book would be a good way for people to get the full picture.

The Future

'One day, in retrospect, the years of struggle will strike you as most beautiful.'

– SF

This is my favourite quote from Freud and one I can truly relate to. It's saying to me that everything I have been through, 'the struggle', has made me a better person. I don't necessarily see the struggle as 'beautiful', but I don't look upon myself negatively for what has happened. The gambling didn't make me happy, but it did drive me towards finding what would make me happy in life. It showed me how important this search was, rather than blindly living my life almost for the sake of it – simply existing.

What would make you happy in life? A question my therapist posed to me during one of our sessions. My answer was simple. I'd like my own house in the countryside with access to woods and fields where I could go walking. My therapist smiled and told me that is achievable. But I know I can't fall back into my old habits.

I no longer feel angry all the time. This feels like a heavy burden which has been lifted from my shoulders and adds to my happiness. I wouldn't want to go backwards ever again and struggle with this emotion, along with the shame. This also opens up avenues for the future as these are feelings which have held me back in the past.

If a fortune teller were sat in front of me reading my future, what would they see? The scariest thought is that we have no control over something. For many years, I have been controlled by my addiction, and what if I will never be able to stop? On the other hand, I also know I have had periods without gambling, periods of happiness. These are the days that keep me going, and for every day I go without succumbing to it, is another day to be thankful for.

A house in the countryside. It sounds perfect.

A Note and Some Acknowledgements

There were a couple of obstacles I had to overcome in writing the book. Firstly, was the decision on whether I wanted to delve into the past – did I want to look back and reflect on the darkest of places I have been? In the end, I decided that writing the book was a positive step in my recovery. The other thing holding me back was the amount of personal memories I would be sharing in writing. In the end, I decided I was happy to let people look at my past. It was part of my path to finding closure. These are things which have happened to me, I cannot alter the story which has already been told and I should not be ashamed. Look at me as the person I am, not as the person I was.

There are a lot of people I would like to thank. People who have kept my head above the water in so many ways, some who probably didn't even know it.

I want to thank my mum and dad first and foremost. Without their support, I'm not sure where I would be today.

I want to thank my sisters. Again, they have always stood by me and most importantly stood by my parents when things were at their worst.

I want to thank my girlfriend. She has had a lot to put up with that no relationship should have to take. She has also driven me to write and finish this book. The number of times I have started something but not finished it is unbelievable.

I want to thank the rest of my family. They never judge me and are always kind.

I want to thank my friends. They make life so easy for me. Some will be reading this having only known part of what's happened over the last 12 years. Some only knew me as the person I wanted to be, someone I want to be all the time now with no secrets. Maybe that's a good thing as I don't expect them to see me as a completely new person.

I want to thank everyone who doesn't know what I've been through and have been there for me without even realising it. People at the gym. People who have written blogs and books to help people like me.

I want to thank my therapists and doctors. You do an amazing job in helping people.

Thanks.